Translated from *Ruta AprendÉxito*. Copyright © Nancy Viana, 2020
*The AprendÉxito Way*. Copyright © Nancy Viana, 2023.
Independent publication by Nancy Viana, 2024.
All rights reserved. San Juan, Puerto Rico.

ISBN 979-8-218-36237-9

**Website:** www.AprendExito.com

EMPRENDE
CON TU LIBRO

**Original Spanish Editor and English Translator:** Yasmín Rodríguez
The Writing Ghost®, Inc.
www.TheWritingGhost.com

**Original Strategic Self-Publishing and Editorial Management Mentor:**
Anita Paniagua
Emprende Con Tu Libro
www.anitapaniagua.com

**Graphic Design and Cover:** Amanda Jusino
www.amandajusino.com

**Author's Photograph:** L. Raúl Romero
raulromerophotography@gmail.com

# Dr. Nancy Viana

## THE AprendÉxito WAY

### A Comprehensive Guide to Unlocking Academic Success

# Testimonies

## This professor breaks all the rules

Dr. Nancy Viana has been instrumental in my development as a social worker. Her main focus is on the well-being and personal growth of her students. Under her guidance, the learning process goes beyond theory, leading to a deeper understanding of reality and self-awareness. Classrooms become therapeutic spaces, aimed at contributing positively to society and providing better service.

*Nahomi M. Velez Balasquide*
Student
Department of Social Work
University of Puerto Rico
Río Piedras Campus

## More than just a professor

As her students, we remember Dr. Nancy Viana as a dedicated protector, a committed warrior, brilliant, perseverant, authentic, and effective. She possesses many other traits that make her more than just a professor. To us, she is the right hand, an example to follow, and the driving force that inspires us to emulate her. Beyond being a professor, she is a true social worker.

*The Nocturnal Eight*
Students
Department of Social Work
University of Puerto Rico
Río Piedras Campus

## Her purpose is to make students rights be heard

I first met Dr. Nancy Viana in August 2001 when I was assigned to work as a special education teacher at the same school where she was employed. Whenever students faced academic learning challenges, Dr. Viana would assist in completing the referral documents to ensure they could undergo evaluation and be enrolled in the program. Through this, she successfully advocated for the rights of the students. Her dedication ensured that our students received exceptional care and support.

*Brenda L. López*
Teacher
Special Education Program

## Her work has been deeply inspiring in my life.

I first met Dr. Viana when I was in elementary school, and she was the school's social worker. During that time, I faced some issues with other students, but Nancy's dedication to promoting equality among all students, ensuring safety, and supporting positive changes made a significant impact on me. Thanks to her support, I was able to overcome my fears and shyness. Her work continues to be a source of inspiration for me. Now, as a psychology student, I aspire to implement the values and lessons I've learned from her in my future endeavors.

*Jonielyz Rivera Reyes*
Student

# Dedication

I dedicate this book to my beloved family, and in particular, to my daughter Francheska, my grandson Fabián, my granddaughter Valentina, my dear father Antonio Viana, and my siblings Edwin, Sonia, Lilly, and Linda. A special mention goes to the person who motivated me to make this dream come true, my dear "George." Thank you all for your unwavering support and love.

Additionally, I dedicate this book to all the children and families who graciously shared their experiences, allowing me to learn and grow as a social worker. Your contributions have been invaluable to my professional development.

With love,
Nancy

# Table of Contents

# I Wrote This Book
# to Help Families

After more than twenty years of experience as a social worker, I decided to write this book to assist families or guardians who lack access to social services and need guidance as they navigate the world of school and its challenges. I hope this methodology serves as the guiding light that accompanies you and the compass that helps you map out the steps to achieve your ultimate goal: your child's academic success.

Another motivation for writing this book is the numerous requests for consultations I have received over the years from parents and professionals seeking alternatives to handle situations during a child's developmental stages, especially throughout the transition from home to school. This transitional process demands specific abilities and knowledge to facilitate the child's full development.

One of the common situations I frequently advise on is the child's entry into the academic environment, which may lead to referrals and complaints from teachers. These situations can affect not only the family but also the child's self-esteem, and they may have lasting impacts on the child's academic and social development.

In this book, I use the term "functional diversity" to address the various needs children may present, which may be referred to as "impediments" or "disabilities" depending on the country and its laws. The term I chose emphasizes acceptance, respect, and dignity for individuals, particularly children, experiencing diverse challenges.

Throughout my career, I have compiled my experiences and knowledge, developing a methodology to strengthen children's capabilities in both academic and family contexts. My *AprendÉxito* methodology is an evaluation system with processes designed to uncover strengths and challenges during the developmental stages, leading to a course of action that ensures success in an academic setting.

This book is for all caregivers of children, including moms, dads, aunts, grandmothers, and guardians, regardless of the children's developmental stage. IT is also for professionals actively working with this population, especially those starting as social work professionals in preschool settings and those currently pursuing their academic training.

I believe this methodology can be a valuable tool for other professionals working with children, such as teachers, speech and language therapists, occupational and physical therapists, and others.

# How Can I Help You?

In this book, I am sharing my professional secrets to pre-pare your child for any educational stage, regardless of the academic route you choose —be it regular public or private education, homeschooling, alternative education, or others.

Drawing on my twenty years of experience as a social worker, focused on children and their families, I present my tried and tested work model that has yielded success-ful results for students at various levels. The *AprendÉxito* method comprises a series of steps to ensure your child is ready to embark on their educational journey. But before we delve into the method, let me explain why it is called *AprendÉxito*. This unique concept combines the Spanish words for learning (*Aprende*) and success (*Éxito*).

*AprendÉxito* is based on the belief that every child can achieve academic success by discovering their individual learning map and leveraging their strengths and capabili-ties for a more independent and fulfilling life. The type of success achieved is for you to determine, and that's why it's essential to chart the appropriate route. The method consists of five roads, each with specific steps leading to different destinations, helping you determine the best course of action for successful outcomes.

This model can be applied from preschool to any educa-tional level or stage. It is founded on prevention, allowing us to address situations proactively before they become problems. Hence, the earlier you integrate the method, the better the results.

*AprendÉxito* facilitates the identification of a child's capabilities and gives special attention to areas that require priority, especially those that need attention before transitioning into a formal education setting. By working on these areas before the child starts school, the results are significantly more beneficial. However, the method can be integrated at any developmental stage if the child is already ahead in their studies.

To make the integration of the *AprendÉxito* method effortless, let's first discuss the evaluation stages. In this section, you will understand the importance of detecting when a child needs help and why it is essential to trust professionals who can guide you to the appropriate assistance.

Once we identify any areas that require support, we can explore different options to aid and guide the child towards a road of success, collaborating with the relevant professionals as a team. Throughout the process, I will share personal anecdotes to illustrate the points I describe. Additionally, you will find tools to adapt the concepts discussed here to your child's specific situation.

# Part #1:

## Evaluating the Child

## Let's Meet the Kid

I vividly recall that morning at a school in my beloved Puerto Rico when a knock on my door interrupted my work in the office of academic social work. To my delight, it was a second-grade student wearing a radiant smile. Let's call him Luis.

As Luis entered, he greeted me warmly, saying, "Good morning, Viana. Over the weekend, I was thinking about something I want to do, and I'm here to ask for one of your hairs. I want to create a clone with your personality and Ricky Martin's!" His words left me utterly surprised, coming from such a young seven-year-old. Luis was bilingual, proficient in both English and Spanish, which he had learned independently through the internet. It was evident that he possessed an intellect that surpassed the norm for his age, making him appear intellectually gifted.

Despite Luis's exceptional intelligence, he faced challenges that hindered his academic and social development. His mother, María, sought help from various professionals in hopes of finding solutions to these difficulties. However, the issues persisted despite their efforts.

During my initial meeting with María, she sought my assistance, feeling confused and despondent. Their journey together had been filled with hardships, including constant school changes in search of an environment where Luis could thrive.

During this meeting, María presented a comprehensive case file she had prepared herself, containing all of Luis's evaluations from his early years up until that moment. The file listed various diagnoses given by other professionals, including epilepsy, Attention-Deficit/Hyperactivity Disorder, depression, and Oppositional Defiant Disorder.

As I reviewed the file, I couldn't help but wonder how a seven-year-old could carry such a heavy burden of labels. What were the implications for him, his family, and his future? The frustration and desperation of a mother uncertain about her child's true struggles became clear to me in that moment. Above all, she worried about how this entire process of searching for answers was affecting Luis, all the while yearning for a solution that could bring them hope and peace, even though it seemed elusive.

Concerning the academic journey, María confided that changing schools and sharing health information caused her immense anxiety, especially when she wasn't entirely clear on the details herself. Recounting her experiences, she noticed that whenever she presented Luis's developmental information to school staff, she would often sense rejection as they swiftly informed her that they lacked the appropriate services for a child like Luis.

Reflecting on the challenges faced by many of our children and their families at the onset of a new educational experience, I couldn't help but recall Luis and his mother, even after all these years. Their situation allowed me to witness firsthand the unfortunate reality that many children and families encounter during this crucial initial stage. It's a phase we typically expect to be joyous, celebrating a child's success.

My work with Luis coincided with the early stages of my professional career, shortly after graduating as a social work major. I had the opportunity to apply the knowledge and skills I gained during my academic training, bridging theory with the participants' reality and eventually developing my own methodology in the process. If you wish to learn more about social work, you can find additional information in the annex section.

Continuing down memory lane, I remember a particular incident in October when I scheduled an initial interview with the mother of a student we'll call Omar. His Kindergarten teacher had referred him to me, concerned about his learning and seeking help to identify the areas where he struggled to grasp the offered skills.

As part of my work at the school, it was agreed that before any students were referred to me, the teachers would keep an anecdotal diary, documenting observations and analyses of the child for at least one month. Additionally, they could integrate test results, completed homework from any subject, evaluations by other professionals, and other relevant sources as secondary information.

Once I had gathered all the necessary data, my second step was to meet with the teacher who initiated the referral. The purpose of this meeting was to discuss and analyze all the information gathered, gaining a better context to establish the subsequent steps to follow. As you can see, social work relies on seeking and compiling information from various perspectives.

In some cases, it became necessary to interview other personnel after speaking with the teacher. For instance, the teacher's assistant or educators responsible for subjects like English, Art, or Physical Education might be included. If relevant, the interview could even extend to some of the colleagues overseeing the school's cleaning and food preparation, as they would be present during the children's mealtimes or recess periods.

Omar was five and a half years old, living with his parents and older siblings. The referral indicated that he faced challenges in activities that required a certain level of independence expected for his grade level. These difficulties included going to the bathroom and eating on his own.

The teacher reported that Omar had trouble using the bathroom independently; he struggled to unbutton his pants, leading to two instances of urinating in his pants. Additionally, he faced difficulties in the lunchroom, requiring assistance to carry his tray and had trouble holding a spoon, affecting his nutrition. These motor skill challenges were impacting his academic performance, particularly in reading and writing, as he found it hard to hold a pencil.

Despite the teacher's efforts to encourage independence through individualized teaching, Omar couldn't achieve these tasks independently. It even seemed that he had difficulty understanding instructions given by the teacher. Other professionals involved in the process confirmed these observations.

Following interviews with school personnel, I spent a day in the classroom solely observing. Subsequently, I arranged a meeting with Omar's family to gain further insight (this investigative role is part of social work tasks and skills). During the interview, we developed a developmental record of Omar, capturing information from his birth until our meeting.

Omar's mother explained that she and her husband cared for him at home until he started Kindergarten. His older siblings, aged 18, 15, and 17, also assisted in his upbringing. Omar held a special place in the family's heart.

Regarding his health, his mother mentioned complications during her sixth month of pregnancy, leading to bed rest and medications. After birth, Omar experienced some medical treatments due to blood type issues, but he was in good physical health until the age of five.

An important aspect of his upbringing was the family's frequent use of a playpen, allowing his caretaker (mainly his father) to manage household tasks. Additionally, Omar typically wore pants with elastic bands, making it easier for him to use the bathroom. However, occasionally, he wore buttoned pants, leading to the need for assistance when using the bathroom.

As our conversation continued, crucial information surfaced. Omar took more time to walk and use the bathroom compared to his siblings. The family had not recognized the extent of the problem until he started school, which was a common occurrence.

To assist Omar, I followed the steps in my methodology. First, we referred him to a pediatrician for a comprehensive evaluation, which went well. Subsequently, his sight and hearing were assessed before referring him to the psychological area.

During the psychological evaluation, professionals identified the need for other assessments, including speech and language, occupational, and physical therapy. After a year of comprehensive analysis, a work plan was developed. This plan incorporated various types of therapy over six years, while also fostering collaboration between the family and school personnel to provide Omar with the necessary tools to enhance his learning capabilities.

## How Do Kids Learn?

As evident in Omar's case, many of his challenges stemmed directly from the sensory stimulation he received during early childhood. Children learn primarily through their senses, which is why they are naturally inclined to touch, see, smell, taste, and hear. As caregivers, it is crucial to be prepared to facilitate this learning process and ensure a safe and enjoyable environment for exploration.

Creating a hazard-free environment allows children to freely explore and learn. During this exploratory phase, they will have numerous questions as they seek to understand the world around them. It is also common for them to imitate the person they are closest to, which is why you might find your child playing with your make-up, trying on your shoes, or even dressing up in your clothes.

Understanding that our children learn through their five senses, it becomes essential for us to know how these senses function. To help you grasp the importance of sensory development, here are some facts about our five senses.

## About the Five Senses and Learning

The five senses are touch, sight, hearing, smell, and taste. It is through these senses that learning takes place. It is essential to know that each person, even identical twins, may have different learning styles. For instance, one of them may learn better through listening, while the other learns through observation and modeling.

In the following table, I include each of the senses, their corresponding body organ, their importance, and some recommendations to enhance learning through each one.

| Sense - organ | Relevance | Recommendations |
|---|---|---|
| **Touch - skin** | It is one of the first senses that develops from the time the baby is in the mother's womb.<br><br>This sense allows the baby to perceive, feel, touch, and become familiar with the surrounding environment. As part of the learning process through touch, there is the identification of:<br>• Textures: hard or soft<br>• Sizes: big or small<br>• Shapes: round or square<br>• Temperature: cold or hot<br><br>The sense of touch can either facilitate or hinder the beginning of writing if not strengthened. For example, it is essential for achieving a good pencil grip, which, in turn, allows the child to make strong and defined letter strokes.<br><br>Touch is also related to the skills needed for walking and other body movements, enabling the child to have mobility and explore the environment around them. | To strengthen skills related to the sense of touch, I recommend the following:<br><br>**Taking care of their skin:**<br>• When your child is exposed to the sun, use child-friendly sunscreen.<br>• After bathing and before bedtime, apply lotion. This not only helps maintain healthy skin but also aids in better sleep. If your child is not allergic, you can incorporate the use of essential oils in creams, such as lavender, which promotes relaxation.<br><br>**Promoting play:**<br>• Engage in activities like playing with play-dough, finger painting, cutting paper with scissors, and tracing drawings. These activities strengthen their fingers and hands, which will assist them in the writing process by improving grip and strokes.<br>• Visit parks that have swings, hanging bars, and slides.<br>• Games like hopscotch, jacks, spinning tops, and marbles are very beneficial for their development.<br>• Board games such as bingo, chess, and dominoes can be integrated with teaching letters and numbers, helping them strengthen social and cognitive skills. |

**Sight – eyes**

It is one of the senses that your child will use the most and a crucial determinant in learning. About 80% of the information your child receives enters through their vision in the form of images and sensations.

Through sight, they can identify colors, sizes, shapes, and the location of objects. Vision allows them to establish a connection with their environment.

In caring for your eyes, it is essential to:

- Use appropriate lighting for reading, especially during homework.
- Limit the use of cell phones, electronic games, and television.
- Maintain a healthy diet.
- Protect the eyes from sun exposure by wearing hats and sunglasses.
- Undergo a yearly visual evaluation to identify any needs in a timely manner.

**Hearing - ears**

Similar to touch, hearing is one of the senses that develops early and is one of the last ones we lose. From the womb, the child can already hear your voice and the voices of people around you.

Hearing allows them to perceive and distinguish sounds in their surroundings, such as recognizing the voices of their mother and grandmother. It facilitates the identification of emotions in other people and, consequently, helps them learn how to respond to those emotions.

I recommend the following:

- When listening to music (with or without head-phones) or using electronic games, ensure they use a moderate volume.
- After activities involving water, such as swimming in pools, rivers, or beaches, make sure to dry the ear area thoroughly.
- Schedule a hearing examination when starting school and periodically as you see fit.

17

| | | |
|---|---|---|
| **Taste - mouth** | The sense of taste is located in the area of the tongue. It allows us to identify different tastes: sweet, salty, bitter, sour, and savory or umami. | To maintain good oral health, it is important to take the child to the dentist for cleanings at least twice a year.<br><br>Use play to enhance learning through this sense:<br><br>• Ask the child to close their eyes and open their mouth, then place a spoonful of banana with yogurt and raisins in it. Ask them, "What did I give you?" |
| **Smell - nose** | This sense facilitates distinguishing odors from different people and things in the environment that surrounds them. | Nasal care involves keeping it clean for proper breathing and free from the introduction of objects.<br><br>During playtime, you can choose various fruits and even sweet spices:<br><br>• Blindfold your child.<br>• Bring a fruit, like an orange, close to their nose. Ask them to try to guess what it is, and do this with each different fruit.<br>• When visiting areas like forests or beaches, ask them to close their eyes and describe the smells they identify and how they perceive them (whether they like them or not, reasons for their response). |

## Children's Developmental Indicators

Developmental indicators are defined as the achievements that most children can reach at a certain stage. To facilitate this presentation, I am including the definition of each indicator, examples of these, recommendations to strengthen each area, a table where you can input data about your child, suggestions on what to do if you identify any needs in any of these areas, and steps of learning, which include additional information about each indicator.

I want to remind you that this exercise offers a general guide to your child's accomplishments. If you have any concerns while completing it, please share them with a qualified professional.

## Developmental Indicators, Exploration, and Learning

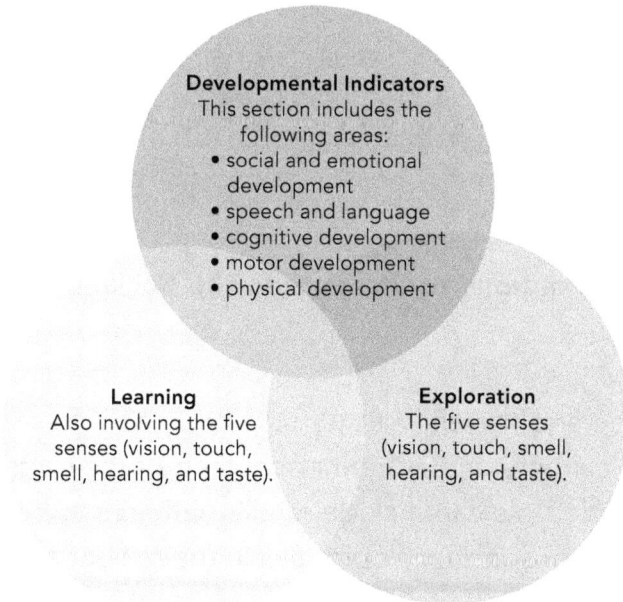

**Developmental Indicators**
This section includes the following areas:
• social and emotional development
• speech and language
• cognitive development
• motor development
• physical development

**Learning**
Also involving the five senses (vision, touch, smell, hearing, and taste).

**Exploration**
The five senses (vision, touch, smell, hearing, and taste).

## Social and Emotional Area

The area of social and emotional development in children refers to the acquisition of skills that enable your child to have friends, cope with frustration, deal with changes, and follow rules of social interaction, among others. This indicator is very important as it is related to mental health.

I recall Iris, a first-grade student who always preferred to be alone and not play, leading many to believe she had issues in the social-emotional area. After being referred for a pediatric evaluation and with the support of a neurologist, it was identified that her behavior was a result of a form of epilepsy that didn't manifest in the usual way. She couldn't express what was happening during her seizures, so she isolated herself from her peers.

Another example I can share is that of Lucy, a second-grade student who would fall asleep in the classroom. She always felt tired and uninterested in playing. When taken to her pediatrician, the doctor identified through a blood test that the girl had a low hemoglobin level.

## Recommendations to Strengthen the Social-Emotional Area

- Encourage the child to participate in activities where they can interact with other children of their age. For example, this can include family gatherings, birthday parties, or special celebrations in their country.

- Based on their interests, guide them to participate in sports teams, art clubs, or other groups.
- Another recommended option, which has proven to be beneficial, is enrolling them in preschool centers.

There are various alternatives available, but it is essential to identify the options that best suit the child's reality: their age, interests, health conditions, and your expectations regarding their development, for example.

## How Can I Discover My Child's Social-Emotional Needs?

Mark with an X in the column that corresponds to the indicator, according to observed experiences.

| Indicator | Always | Under way | Never |
|---|---|---|---|
| Wants to please their friends | | | |
| Wants to be like their friends | | | |
| Can follow rules or guidelines | | | |
| Likes singing, dancing and/or acting | | | |
| Can recognize other people's gender | | | |
| Distinguishes fantasy from reality | | | |
| Shows independence | | | |

## What Should I Do if I Identify a Need in This Area?

If you have access to the services of a social worker at the school or preschool center, that should be one of your first options. They will analyze the situation and establish an action plan for the benefit of the child, which may include services such as interviews, support, coordination, and referrals to other professionals, as well as information on developmental stages and other relevant areas.

### Learning Steps

When we hear the term "mental health", an alarm goes off, as there are many prejudices about what it is and how it relates to our children. I share with you the following definition: "Mental health in childhood and early childhood refers to the child's early relationships and their social and emotional development." (Connecticut Child Health and Development Institute)

When we talk about mental health in early childhood, we refer to the ability to:

- Experience affectionate and responsive relationships with their caregivers
- Build relationships with others
- Explore and learn
- Communicate through play
- Express and regulate their emotions

To this I add the five social-emotional learning (SEL) competencies from the Collaborative for Academic, Social, and Emotional Learning (CASEL). These competencies are developed throughout life and can be introduced from early ages. The five SEL competencies are:

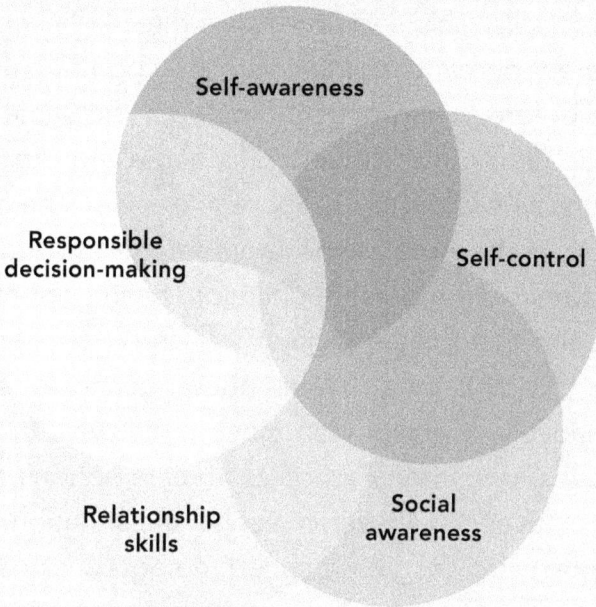

Self-awareness

Responsible
decision-making

Self-control

Relationship
skills

Social
awareness

- **Self-awareness:** It consists of identifying one's own emotions and accepting them, in a way that facilitates the achievement of accurate self-perception, recognizing their strengths, and building self-confidence and self-efficacy. For example, there is a movie that I like to use a lot with children called Inside Out, which presents the main emotions such as joy, sadness, fear, anger, and disgust. It's a great opportunity to watch it together and ask the child if they have ever felt these types of emotions and how they were able to handle them. Likewise, we can share our own examples of experiencing similar emotions. This way, the child can identify when they feel joy, but also develop the ability to identify when they feel anger or frustration and the event that caused it.

- **Self-control:** It is the ability that children acquire to manage their impulses, handle stress, self-discipline, self-motivate, set goals, and demonstrate organizational skills. This competency is directly linked to the previous one since the first step is recognizing the emotion before taking action. However, the same movie, Inside Out, provides examples of making positive decisions when feeling emotions like anger. The decision made in the heat of the moment can have negative outcomes if the person (or child) doesn't self-regulate. A technique for self-regulation can be counting from one to ten to give time for the anger to subside. Alternatively, a person can close their eyes, take deep breaths, and then recognize their emotions and the alternatives they have to resolve the situation. For example: when Sergio is pushed, he gets angry and yells at people. One day, he was pushed in his classroom, and he was about to yell, but he remembered what his teacher had told him and chose to count from one to ten. This helped his emotion decrease in intensity. Finally, he asked his classmate about what happened and learned that it was unintentional, because the classmate had tripped and accidentally pushed him.

- **Social awareness:** It involves accepting and embracing diversity, showing empathy, and being able to regulate emotions, thoughts, and actions. It's when a child can recognize the feelings and perspectives of others, as well as individual and group similarities and differences. For example: Lucy doesn't have pets because she doesn't like them, but when Sully's little dog passed away, Lucy hugged Sully to express her support and empathy for her friend's sadness.

- **Relationship skills:** It involves establishing and maintaining interpersonal relationships, possessing social awareness, being empathetic, accepting and embracing diversity, showing interest in understanding others, and being willing to approach and help others if needed. It also means learning both to listen and to ask for help when necessary. It's when a child can responsibly apply their skills to deal with the social and school situations they face daily. For example: Marta went to buy candies at the school store and noticed that Miss Luisa was sitting there, crying. Marta approached her and asked what was wrong, and Miss Luisa said she was feeling unwell. The girl quickly ran to find the school principal to ask for help for Miss Luisa.

- **Responsible decision-making:** It involves responsibly evaluating decisions, the ability to work in a team, establishing and maintaining positive and healthy relationships, and managing and resolving conflicts. It's the capacity to assess the possible consequences of our actions or behaviors, as well as making decisions based on values and ethical standards. It is demonstrated when there is an ability to prevent, manage, and resolve interpersonal conflicts appropriately. For example: William had to do a group assignment for his English class, and he wanted his twin brother, Marcelo, to be part of his group. However, the teacher assigned Marcelo to another group. At first, William was a little shy because he didn't know the other children in his group, but after a few minutes, he integrated with them and helped identify the objects the teacher asked them to select on the sheet, which led them to arrive in first place in the game.

## Speech and Language Area

In the speech and language area, it is expected that a child has the ability to communicate moods, feelings, emotions, and experiences. Language enables and facilitates interactions with others and the sharing of information.

As you can see, this area consists of two words: "speech" and "language." These concepts are not the same, although they are closely related. Communication through language refers to the exchange of information between two individuals: the one conveying the message and the one receiving it. So, speech is the way your child communicates, using language with their voice to convey the intended message. Speech is the means, and communication through language is the end or purpose to be achieved.

As part of the indicators of speech and communication, it is expected that the child can follow simple and slightly more complex verbal commands, such as "come with me" or "I need you to help me pick up all the toys and put them in their drawers." Additionally, the child should be able to count to ten or more and pronounce most words correctly. Another important indicator is their ability to name all common objects that are part of their culture, as well as parts of their body.

In the case of Josefa's son, who is four years old, he speaks softly and his pronunciation of letter sounds is unclear, making it difficult for his family to understand what he says. To determine if the child indeed has a speech problem, Josefa should visit a pediatrician for an evaluation, and if necessary, the pediatrician may refer the child to a specialized professional in this area, such as a speech-language pathologist. I would recommend that she also consider visiting an audiologist before the speech and language evaluation.

**Recommendations to Strengthen the Speech and Language Area**

You can take advantage of almost all activities you do with your child to strengthen this area. For example, when bathing, you can ask them to name body parts as they soap themselves or play a guessing game about body parts. This way, you teach them the correct names.

Another game, suitable for children who have started working with the alphabet, is the game "I spy." Here's an example of it:
- I spy with my little eye.
- What do you see?
- A little thing.
- What letter does it start with?
- With the letter "n."
- Nose.

Finally, I recommend that you place cards with the names of objects and areas around the house, such as "clock," "bed," "kitchen," "bathroom." This way, the child will start to associate letters, words, and their meanings.

### How Can I Discover My Child's Speech and Language Needs?

Mark with an X in the column that corresponds to the indicator, according to observed experiences.

| Indicator | Always | Under way | Never |
|---|---|---|---|
| Talks clearly | | | |
| Can tell a complete story using full sentences | | | |
| Can use future tense in conversations | | | |
| Can say their name and address | | | |

### What Should I Do if I Identify a Need in This Area?

Visit the social worker if you have access to one. Additionally, you can talk to the teacher if the child is attending a school or learning center. Likewise, you can visit your pediatrician.

### Learning Steps

It is essential to have a physical evaluation by the pediatrician before starting any other assessments. Once the pediatrician identifies if there is any need, they will make the appropriate referral, either to a speech-language pathologist or an audiologist if they suspect the child may have hearing loss affecting their speech pronunciation.

## Cognitive Area

In the cognitive area, you can find indicators of your child's learning, reasoning, and problem-solving abilities. Learning is the capacity to acquire new knowledge and apply it in daily life. Reasoning is what allows them to analyze that information and leads them to take actions. We can observe reasoning when they face a problem and identify alternatives to solve it.

Luis is in kindergarten, and his teacher has told all the students that when they have any situation with a classmate, they need to talk to her or the assistant. One day, José took the money Luis had for his snack without permission, and Luis hit him with his bag. The teacher scolded Luis for hitting José.

This is an example of how important it is for children to learn to make the right decisions and follow agreements or rules that are important for coexistence. In that situation, it was appropriate for Luis to tell the teacher what happened, so she could talk to José. This is a learning process that sometimes takes time, but it's important to be consistent with our rules at home so that when they are in other environments, the transition is facilitated.

## Recommendations to Strengthen the Cognitive Area

It is important to expose children to new experiences that facilitate learning while engaging in various activities. Play is a natural and effective way for them to acquire knowledge. Families can create enjoyable activities integrating different games like bingo, ball games, dominoes, Scrabble, and more, depending on the child's stage of development and existing knowledge.

Considering that technology plays a significant role in modern life, identifying apps that promote cognitive development, teamwork, and the ability to follow precise instructions can be beneficial. It is also essential to monitor and control screen time to strike a balance in their activities.
Families can organize competitions and tournaments for games like dominoes, fostering family bonding and fun. Another lovely tradition is a yearly ball game involving all family members, from grandparents to grandchildren.

Additionally, encouraging children to participate in age-appropriate groups, such as scouting, preschool centers, art, and music groups, can provide valuable learning experiences and opportunities to interact with peers in diverse settings.

## How Can I Discover My Child's Cognitive Needs?

Mark with an X in the column that corresponds to the indicator, according to observed experiences.

| Indicator | Always | Under way | Never |
|---|---|---|---|
| Counts up to ten or more | | | |
| Can draw a person with at least six correct body parts | | | |
| Can write some letters or numbers | | | |
| Can duplicate triangles and other geometrical shapes | | | |
| Understands how to use money | | | |
| Knows most of their body parts (head, legs, arms, etc.) | | | |

## What Should I Do if I Identify a Need in This Area?

You can go to the social worker, express your concern, and share it with the teachers. Also, you should take the child for a pediatric evaluation to ensure everything is alright. Finally, you can visit a psychologist. I always recommend getting pediatric, vision, and hearing evaluations done before a psychological assessment. Sometimes, depending on the analysis of the situation, I refer to a neurologist to rule out aspects in this area, such as epilepsy.

## Learning Steps

Child development is a continuous evolution, and I am sharing a table of the developmental areas: motor, cognitive, language, and social, which will help you identify the stage of development your child is in.

## Developmental Table for Children from Zero to Six Years (adapted from GuiaInfantil.com):

| Develop-mental Areas | 0 - 6 months | 6 - 12 months | 1 - 2 years | 2 - 4 years | 4 - 6 years |
|---|---|---|---|---|---|
| Motor | Lifts head Prepares for crawling | Crawls Stands and takes a few steps | Walks Learns to climb stairs | Learns to climb stairs Learns to ride a bicycle or skateboard | Jumps, climbs skillfully, and enjoys dancing |
| Cognitive | Attends to visual and auditory stimuli | Has a favorite toy Increases independence and curiosity | Shows more interest in books and toys | Shows more interest in drawing | Refines drawing skills, dresses independently, gains more autonomy |
| Language | Communicates through crying and smiling Babbling | Says first words | Begins to combine words, but makes frequent mistakes | Language is nearly perfect, but may have difficulty with some sounds or stuttering | Able to express emotions and thoughts |
| Social | Depends on family members | Shows more interest in groups | Becomes less attached to parents and seeks to play with other children | The "why" and tantrum stage | Enjoys group games |

## Motor and Physical Development Area

Physical development involves significant changes in motor development, such as the acquisition of basic motor skills: walking, running, jumping, climbing, throwing, catching, among others. Motor development, in which humans acquire a vast array of motor skills, occurs through the progression from simple and disorganized movements to organized and complex motor skills.

Motor skills represent solutions to children's goals. When they feel motivated to achieve something, they can create a new motor behavior. The new behavior results from various factors: the development of the nervous system, the physical properties of the body and its movement capabilities, the goal the child is motivated to achieve, and the support from the environment (Premium Madrid, Global Health Care, 2016).

In Omar's situation, we can clearly see how his motor development was affected, since unbuttoning his pants is a skill that develops as part of his process of independence. These skills are acquired through the development and exposure to different stimuli.

We know that Omar, his father, and his mother were not aware of the importance of developing this skill. The result of this skill not being developed is that other skills are affected in turn, as well as his overall learning process.

**Recommendations to Strengthen the Motor and Physical Development Area**

On many occasions, our children seem like whirlwinds, as a happy child is always on the move, going up and down without direction. This is part of their nature and development, as children develop physical skills in a certain order. For example, they crawl first, then walk, and later run.

That's why I recommend helping them strengthen these skills with the following activities: pushing objects like a box, pulling a rope, walking in the yard or park, throwing and catching balls, climbing in designated areas such as those known as rappelling spots, to give you some examples. This way, we can reintroduce activities like climbing trees, which have sometimes been lost due to excessive caution or overprotection of our children.

It's good to find a balance in this regard. They can also engage in activities like maintaining balance while walking in a straight line. What child doesn't enjoy a race? This is the perfect time to coordinate a family race, and you can even play the "dwarf and giant" jumping game. During summer vacations, encourage swimming and activities where they can move their feet in the water (Babycenter, 2019).

I recommend continuing to expose and encourage your child to participate in different activities. For instance, on the website "Nuts and Neurons" (2017) by Dr. Sandra Cid Sillero, there are some tips for achieving effective writing skills in children, as this is a process that develops gradually:

- Drawing with various materials, such as sand, finger paint, using brushes, different sizes of crayons (starting with thicker ones).
- Painting, cutting, doing puzzles, mazes, and connecting dots with numbers.
- Practicing vertical, horizontal, and circular strokes, etc.
- Teaching the child to hold the pencil correctly, how to grip and glide it over the paper. Initially, this can be achieved with a thicker pencil, and then progress to thinner ones.

## How Can I Discover My Child's Motor and Physical Development Needs?

Mark with an X in the column that corresponds to the indicator, according to observed experiences.

| Indicator | Always | Under way | Never |
|---|---|---|---|
| Stands on one foot for ten seconds or more | | | |
| Jumps and can move forward with short hops, alternating between one foot and the other | | | |
| Can do somersaults | | | |
| Uses a fork and spoon for eating, and occasionally a knife | | | |
| Can go to the bathroom alone | | | |
| Swings | | | |
| Can climb | | | |

## What Should I Do if I Identify a Need in This Area?

If after reading and analyzing your child's physical and motor development aspects, you want to ensure that they are meeting the expected milestones for their age, you can use the following resources:

- Visit your social worker, as besides listening to your concerns and providing support, they can connect you with other professionals.

- You can also go to your pediatrician and share your concerns, so they can conduct their evaluation and determine if your child is indeed within the expected parameters. If not, they may refer you to another professional, likely in the field of psychology. Psychological assessments include areas related to motor skills, and they may recommend an evaluation in physical therapy or occupational therapy, for example.

## Learning Steps

Among the Centers for Disease Control and Prevention (2019) recommendations, they include being alert when our child:

___ Does not express a wide range of emotions
___ Displays extreme behaviors (excessive fear, aggression, shyness, or sadness)
___ Is overly withdrawn or passive
___ Is easily distracted and has difficulty concentrating on an activity for more than five minutes
___ Does not respond to people or does so in a limited way
___ Cannot distinguish between fantasy and reality
___ Lacks a variety of games and activities
___ Cannot say their first and last name
___ Does not use plurals and past tense correctly
___ Does not talk about their daily activities or experiences
___ Does not draw
___ Cannot brush their teeth
___ Cannot wash and dry their hands
___ Cannot undress without help
___ Regresses and loses previously acquired skills.

## We Discovered Your Child. Now What?

I remember that day when I found Carmen alone, crying in front of the school library, covering her face with her hands. This happened because she was frustrated with her son Freddy, who couldn't stay inside the classroom but instead ran around the school. Carmen had a mix of emotions, including shame, sadness, anger, and even feeling guilty for her son's behavior. This situation caused her distress about Freddy's safety and also affected his learning, as he couldn't complete his tasks.

At that moment, I gently placed my hand on her shoulder and said, "I'm here for you, you are not alone." She cried even more, so I gave her time to handle that mix of emotions. Later, we went to my office, where she talked about the frustration she felt as the semester was about to end, and she couldn't get her son to follow the instructions given at school and at home. Completing tasks was a challenge.

This story reflects the reality that many mothers and fathers experience when their children start school because this new environment requires social skills that facilitate their transition and learning. Now, when should we seek help? Where do we start? The answers to these questions depend on your child's needs and the availability of services within your reach.

Using the presented situation as a starting point, the child was enrolled in a school that offered different programs and professionals: a regular education program (for all children), a special education program (for children with identified educational needs), a library that provided services of special projects integrated into classes, homework support, and the services of a social worker specializing in families and children.

The school also had a team of professionals that offered therapies for children with speech and communication needs, occupational therapy, psychological therapy, and food services (breakfast and lunch).

In many cases, as a social worker, it is necessary to give the mother or father time and space to process their thoughts, emotions, and actions in response to the information presented. They have to deal with many pressures and emotions, including the stigma and prejudices faced by many children and adults with functional diversity.

Sometimes, I would compare the process that parents were going through with the stages of grief management presented by psychiatrist Elizabeth Kubler Ross in 1969: denial, anger, bargaining, depression, and acceptance.

For instance, when the teacher would meet with parents and present that their child was struggling to read or comprehend what they read, parents would seek reasons to justify this, saying things like, "But he reads at home," which might be true, but the specific skill the teacher needed to assess was not being achieved. This situation posed a threat to their child and led to frustration for parents because, as I mentioned earlier, our expectation is to see our children shine and succeed at school, not to face frustrations and sad events.

On other occasions, parents directed anger at the school, some of us, God, or anything that could help justify the situation. For example, we encountered situations where parents verbally expressed their frustration and anger. As I understood it, I sought ways to validate those feelings, knowing they were temporary and would eventually lead to apologies, as it happened on more than one occasion. The stage of depression was evident when the evaluation results came in. This stage was marked by hopelessness and sadness, often arising from how academic performance was being affected while trying to figure out the underlying problem.

The stage of bargaining would occur when denial and anger had been overcome, and parents began seeking solutions, which might have been offered at the beginning. For instance, they would return to ask for help in identifying a psychologist or pediatrician to start that process. Finally, acceptance would come once we had a clear understanding of the situation, the reasons behind their child's academic struggles, and parents would comprehend the results while also identifying alternatives for collaborative work.

Given that every child is different, with unique needs and strengths, I can say the way we handle these situations varies from person to person. Hence, my message is this: you have the right to express your emotions and feelings about the situation you are facing, and no one should dictate how you should feel since this is a highly individual experience.

You don't have to feel the way others feel, and you don't have to be like other people. We all have different ways of handling our emotions and feelings, and you need time and space to do so. So, whenever you need it, it's your right.

The process of empowering parents to deal with situations they hadn't considered takes time. Internalizing that what I now see as a limitation or challenge for myself and my child will eventually transform, and that the child will have greater strengths, is not immediate.

Returning to Carmen's situation, the process of identifying her son's needs for improvement had already started, but the strategies used were not working entirely. She wasn't ready yet to reach the stage of acceptance, which occurs once we acknowledge that something is happening.

As part of this stage, Carmen requested to volunteer at the school and be closer to her child, especially regarding his safety. She worried that during one of his escapades from the classroom or during lunchtime, something might happen. Although we knew that might not be the best solution, we gave her that time to go through this process. At that moment, her son only received services from the regular program, and to be eligible for other services, there was a process of referrals, evaluations, and discussions with the team to eventually establish a plan.

These processes of identifying needs and providing services take quite some time. I had situations that could take a year, and others, even more than that. It all depends on the complexity of the situation and the availability of services.

# Part #2:

## And Now, What Do I Do With My Child?

## Let's Start the Path to Academic Success

I will share with you the methodology called *AprendÉxi-to*, which I developed over the years while working with preschool and school-age children, as they face challenges during the transition process. *AprendÉxito* facilitates the identification of their strengths and the capacities that are still in development and require special attention. This way, we can focus on fulfilling both the child's and their family's educational expectations.

This methodology is based on the UNICEF Convention on the Rights of the Child, as human rights aspects play a vital role in social work:

- Ensuring the right to survive and maintain health
- Promoting the right to education
- Encouraging the right to play
- Providing protection rights
- Preserving the right not to separate from their families
- Acknowledging the right to have a name
- Valuing the right to express opinions and be heard

Another crucial element of this methodology involves integrating bio-psycho-social aspects, with the active involvement of other professionals. Bio-psycho-social aspects form a widely utilized model in different disciplines, allowing us to view and analyze individuals holistically (completely, not from a single dimension). These aspects can be divided into the following areas:

- Biological (physical health)
- Psychological (thinking and learning)
- Social (relationships)

To grasp the children's progress in each of these areas, other professionals actively participate in the evaluation process. For example, a pediatrician takes part in the biological area to assess the child's physical health situation. In the psychological area, a professional in this field collaborates, and a social worker addresses aspects related to the child's relationships and environment. Depending on the situations, other professionals, like neurologists or occupational therapists, can also get involved in each of these three areas.

To understand how children are doing in each of these areas, other professionals actively participate in the evaluation process. For example, in the biological area, a pediatrician is involved to assess the child's physical health situation. In the psychological area, a professional in this field is integrated, and a social worker addresses aspects related to the child's relationships and environment. Depending on the situations, other professionals, like neurologists or occupational therapists, can be integrated into each of these three areas.

In this book, I adapt this methodology for you, so it can serve as a guide to support your child, especially if you want to ensure they are ready to enter the schooling process. *AprendÉxito* is useful for any stage of development, including adulthood.

It's important to clarify that your child's educational center may not have a methodology like this, so it's a great opportunity to provide this information to the school staff. The important thing is to take that first step towards transforming processes for the well-being of your child, as well as others.

But what is *AprendÉxito*? It is a procedure that involves a series of steps, which, in turn, establish the activities you need to carry out to achieve the desired result. Besides these steps, there are other components that form the backbone of the methodology and will help you follow it. These are aspects you will need to strengthen as a mother, father, or caregiver to succeed alongside your child because it is a teamwork effort.

Before we delve into the steps of the methodology, I need your commitment to carry out this procedure. In other words, I want you to accept working with this methodology because you believe in it and want the best for your child. This requires your commitment to start and finish this process, knowing that moments that test us may arise along the way.

To make this journey more bearable, I wish you the power of faith. From faith comes the hope of achieving a better future for your child, as it has been my compass. Faith will strengthen your mind and give you the power that no one can take away from you: the hope that success awaits you beyond the horizon. Always visualize in your mind the image you wish to have at the end of our work. Through this book, you will have me as an ally, and you will not be alone.

Also, I wish you the power of persistence. This power provides you with perseverance, which has helped me reach the goal with my students. Persistence will allow you to continue identifying alternatives and helps you have greater endurance. It's like athletes running long marathons with the necessary energy to reach the finish line, despite obstacles or barriers along the way.

Finally, you will need the gift of assertive communication. With this, you can communicate your child's needs clearly and precisely, getting straight to the point. For example, you can say, "Good morning, doctor. I greatly appreciate the service you provide to my child. He is starting school this year, so I would like to ensure that he is ready to learn. That's why I brought him to you, to ensure he is in good health and also that he can see well."

Assertive communication will open the doors to understanding with other people, to whom you will need to communicate your child's needs as clearly as possible. Many people may seem to listen, but they don't fully grasp the needs. That's why I always present my needs in a concrete way, and I recommend that you practice doing the same with your child's needs. No one knows better than you what he needs.

Regarding referrals, as a mother or father, you must consent to their content and sending, as they will express part of what was discussed in the interview with the social worker.

The pediatrician can also provide you with referrals to other professionals. For example, if they identify that the child doesn't see well, they will refer him for a vision evaluation. However, since my methodology is based on prevention, if they don't offer referrals, you will request the necessary ones.

Now, I am going to present to you the *AprendÉxito* route for parents and caregivers. Allow me to walk this journey with you, step by step.

# THE
# AprendÉxito

WAY

# Road #1:

## Identify the Geographical Point

In this phase, we will identify where your child stands on the development map to begin the *AprendÉxito* route. You can take all your notes for each step in a separate notebook designated for this purpose, or in the annex *My AprendÉxito Table.*

**Step 1: Referral or Concern**

This stage begins with a referral or concern, either from yourself, a family member, or a professional who attends to your child, such as the teacher. I invite you to answer the following questions.

• What is my concern or the concern brought to me about my child?

_____
_____
_____
_____

• Who is the concern coming from?

_____
_____
_____
_____

- When was it identified?

_____

_____

_____

_____

- How does this affect my child?

_____

_____

_____

_____

- What are the outcomes of this situation for my child?

_____

_____

_____

_____

- What outcomes could it have if I do not address this concern?

_____

_____

_____

_____

## Step 2: Organize Your File and Add Information

For the second step, I invite you to start organizing a file for the child. You can do this with a folder or envelope you have at home. Include all the documents you have available, such as birth certificate, social security card, health records, school documents like report cards, among others. If the child is in any educational system, gather all their reports, from the beginning until the present.

Additionally, in this step, I invite you to add information using the development indicators questionnaires and the history appendix included at the end of the book. Include any other necessary information and any additional questions that may arise.

## Step 3: Analyze and Write What You Understand to Be the Issue (Concern)

Personally, I don't like using the term "problem"; I prefer to call it a "concern." But I know it's easier to identify it using the term "problem."

But before analyzing it, let's define it.

The problem refers to the gap between the current situation represented in the concern or referral and what you, as a family, including your child, would expect it to be.

To accurately identify the problem and its causes, we need to gather relevant information about it to identify possible alternatives to resolve it. Let's begin the search for relevant information related to this problem or concern.

# Road #2:

## Start the *AprendÉxito* Way
## With the Universal Stops

Where does my road start? I know this is the question that comes to your mind: where do I start in order to help my child? My first recommendation is to follow each of these *AprendÉxito* route steps, so we can reach the final destination through the right path. As we make the journey, we will map out the route, and you'll be jotting down everything that happens, including dates, milestones, and any doubts.

## Step 1: Universal Stops

Let's start the *AprendÉxito* way with the three universal stops: pediatrician, audiologist, and optometrist. I suggest we coordinate the date for the first stop on this route, which will be the appointment with the pediatrician. Once we finish the pediatric evaluation, we'll schedule the second stop, which is the audiological evaluation. Lastly, we'll arrange the third and final stop on the *AprendÉxito* way, which is the visual evaluation. In the chapter "*Establishing Your Personal Route*," we will explore the universal stops in detail.

## Step 2: Analyze Your Route

The second step of this stage is to analyze the results of the universal stops. What were the outcomes of the evaluations? Did you receive any recommendations? Did you obtain any answers to those questions?

Please write down the answers and any questions or doubts you may have.

_____

_____

_____

_____

_____

_____

_____

_____

_____

Let's see if, with these new results, we can address some of the questions that came up during Step 1. Based on your response, we will make a decision.

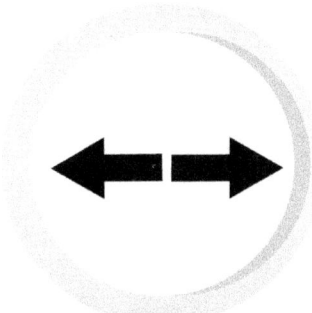

# Road #3:

## Analyze the *AprendÉxito* Way Taken

## Step 1: Analyze and React

In this first step of the third phase, we already have the results of the pediatric, visual, and audiological evaluations, and you recorded them along with the recommendations in the *AprendÉxito* table or your notebook.

- What were the results of each evaluation: pediatric, audiological, and visual?

_____

_____

_____

_____

- Did they offer any recommendations that require immediate action? For example, purchasing prescription glasses or hearing aids.

_____

_____

_____

_____

- What did I find on the universal route?

_____

_____

_____

_____

• What do I still not understand or have clear?

_____
_____
_____
_____

• What are my child's strengths?

_____
_____
_____
_____

• What are the areas or capacities in development?

_____
_____
_____
_____

• Which ones need to be addressed with priority?

_____
_____
_____
_____

• Do I have all the necessary information to make decisions?

_____
_____
_____
_____

- What were the recommendations?

_____

_____

_____

_____

- Why these results?

_____

_____

_____

_____

- Do I have additional referrals?

_____

_____

_____

_____

- Did they recommend visiting any specific professional and provided their contact information?

_____

_____

_____

_____

- Was I able to clarify my doubts with the professionals who evaluated my child?

_____

_____

_____

_____

- Is there still something that is not clear to me?

_____

_____

_____

_____

Try to answer any questions that come up, as this will help you move on to the next step, which is decision-making, where you will evaluate the alternatives based on the results.

## Step 2: Decision-Making

The second step of this third phase is to decide whether we will finish the *AprendÉxito* way or, on the contrary, we need to plan the next stops.

And how do we know which decision to make? To assist you in this process, I invite you to read about the next stops: psychologist, speech and language, occupational therapy, and neurological therapy.

In each of these stops, I narrate a story that may resemble your child's, which will help you choose the next stop. I also explain in general terms what to expect from this professional and how they can help your child. Once you finish reviewing all the information, you will choose between the two alternatives: finish the route or continue.

## Alternative 1: You Completed the Route

If you choose this alternative, it's because no further evaluations, treatments, or therapeutic services were recommended at the universal stops. In other words, everything went well.

You can also complete the route if, for example, they identified that your child needed glasses, which have already been obtained, and the concern or problem has been resolved. For instance, your child can now write everything and doesn't leave sentences incomplete.

## Alternative 2: Continue the Route

Now, if you were offered specific recommendations to conduct one or more evaluations for the child, you may decide to continue with the *AprendÉxito* way.

You can also choose to continue the *AprendÉxito* way after completing the universal stops if, despite your child being prescribed glasses (thinking that was the problem) and using them for approximately a month, the original issue persists.

In this case, new questions arise. For example, if your child already has glasses, what could be happening? Based on my experience, I would recommend a visit to a psychologist as the next stop. I am confident that they could be of assistance.

# Road #4:

## Plan Your Personal *AprendÉxito* Route

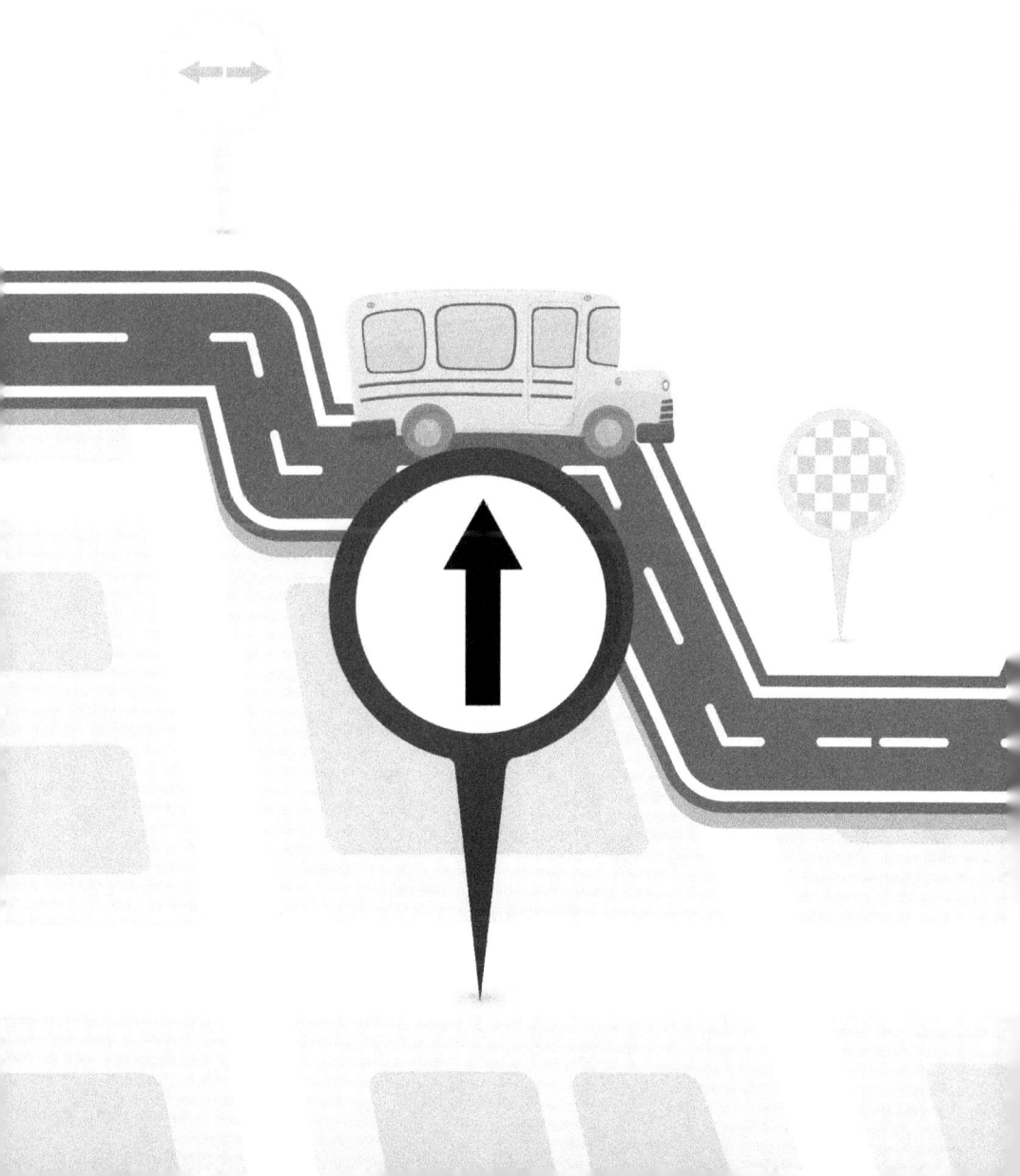

If you reached this phase, it means you identified that your child needs to continue the *AprendÉxito* route. In this phase, we will follow these steps: I identify and write, set the goal, and assign a value.

You received several recommendations, which led to questions such as: What are the stops along the *AprendÉxito* way? Which stop should we start with? Where can I find these specialists? How much will each evaluation cost?

## Step 1: Identify and Write

You have the evaluations from the universal stops at hand. This analysis allows you to establish the areas of needs or developing capacities of the child, as well as the priorities.

What were the results of road #3? Reanalyze everything: the referral, the documents you have in the record, and the results of the pediatric, audiological, and visual evaluations.

What are the recommendations? Make a list in the table included in the *My AprendÉxito Table* appendix or write them down in your notebook. In the next step, we will establish the priorities.

## Step 2: Establish the Goal

To establish the plan, we need to develop a goal and answer some questions. What do I want to do? How do I want to do it? By when do I want to do it? Who can help me achieve it?

Here's an example of a goal: I want my child to improve his reading comprehension through speech and language therapy and continue developing his knowledge according to his chronological age.

Write your goal, and it can be more than one.

## Step 3: Assign Value

Which stop should I do first? Were any specific recommendations given to me to do one stop before another? After noting the recommendations provided in each evaluation of the universal stops, I invite you to establish the importance, or value, of each one. For example, if you have three recommendations, which could represent three additional stops with different specialists, you will decide which one should be addressed first, the second, and then the third. Write down the reasons for establishing this order.

## Step 4: Identify and Coordinate

Now, let's identify the professionals who can help you and coordinate the stops or visits. Where can I find those professionals that were recommended to me? What health insurance do I have? What alternatives are available in my geographical area?

### Identify

First, prepare a list of potential professionals who provide the recommended services. Let's start by identifying the services available under the state or government health services.

Secondly, let's search for the list of service providers covered by your private health insurance, if you have one.

Thirdly, identify other alternatives such as those available at universities or higher education institutions, as well as non-profit organizations. Some of them offer free and high-quality services to the community.

### Coordinate

Review the recommendation before making the call related to it. When you introduce yourself, mention that you are interested in scheduling a visit. Remember to ask any questions you may have, such as: Does the child need to fast? Should we bring the eyeglasses? How long does the visit take? Should I bring food for the child? Is it cold at the location? Prior to any of the upcoming appointments, if the use of eyeglasses or hearing aids was recommended, for example, it's important to bring them along.

• Prepare a list of possible recommended professionals:

_____

_____

_____

_____

• Check the list of service providers under your health insurance:

_____

_____

_____

_____

• Identify other alternatives such as universities, non-profit organizations, and other service providers:

_____

_____

_____

_____

• Coordinate appointments and visits with the selected professionals:

_____

_____

_____

_____

_____

_____

Always go back to the *My AprendÉxito Table* annex and write your notes. Now, let's go into the last phase.

# Road #5:

## Arrival Point of the *AprendÉxito* Route

In this phase, repeat your analysis after receiving evaluations and services. Now what? Has the problem been resolved? Have we achieved the goal? What else do we need?

Let's analyze the results of all the roads and stops along the AprendÉxito way, comparing the changes before and after the journey. Engage in conversations with the people in contact with the child again: teachers, therapists, and others, and ask them about their observations. Depending on the child's progress, you may identify new recommendations to integrate into the process.

## Step 1: Evaluate the Roads and Stops Along the AprendÉxito Way

During this step, let's revisit all the roads and their stops once again. Let's recall the initial problem you identified and the goal you set for your child's development. Now, let's examine the results of the stops along the *AprendÉxito* way. The key question is, did your child's developmental progress improve? We hope to see positive changes that align with both your aspirations and your child's own goals. By evaluating the outcomes and engaging with teachers, therapists, and others involved, we can identify further recommendations and continue to refine the process.

## Step 2: What's Next

Congratulations! If everything went well and you achieved your goal successfully, then you have completed the route. Sometimes, there may be a need to revisit a stop, but it could be a brief one. Remember to stay motivated and optimistic, as that is crucial on this journey.

Keep moving forward, you are going to make it! Don't give up!

# Establish Your Own Journey

## Three Universal Stops

### First Stop – Pediatric Evaluation

The first stop on the way for every child, regardless of their age and needs, is the pediatrician's office or primary care doctor. I recommend that, whenever possible, you keep the child with the same doctor. This helps maintain a chronology of their development, enabling a better analysis of their needs.

This initial visit is crucial, as before evaluating other areas, we need to ensure that your child's biological area (physical health) is in good condition. Once we are assured of their good health, we can move on to the next areas.

I remember a student named Joselo who, after several visits to his pediatrician and with the support of another specialist known as a neurologist (a medical professional specializing in the nervous system), managed to identify that the problem he had was not attention deficit disorder (ADD) or "laziness." Instead, he was diagnosed with "epileptic absence seizures."

None of us had thought that this condition was affecting his learning. Additionally, it was discovered that he also had hypoglycemia (low blood sugar), which I will explain further in this same section.

Joselo was in first grade when his teacher referred him because his learning was well below expectations. The teacher mentioned that he exhibited good behavior in the classroom but had poor interpersonal relationships, hardly engaging in play and often isolating himself. Although he seemed to be listening and observing everything presented during the day, he struggled with reading, writing, and especially mathematical processes.

After conducting interviews, we initiated the referral and evaluation process, culminating in the diagnosis of epileptic absence seizures. It was my first experience with this condition, and I had to read about it since the epilepsy I was familiar with was different.

This absence seizure is characterized by the child zoning out for a few seconds, which is why he missed parts of the mathematical process and couldn't arrive at the correct answer.

According to the Kids Health website, during such a seizure, the child may stare blankly or blink repeatedly, making it difficult for the teacher to notice that the child is experiencing a silent seizure. Considering that these seizures can occur up to 100 times a day and last for three to fifteen seconds each, one can imagine how much educational material the child was missing out on.

### What does pediatrics entail?

Sometimes, we might assume that any doctor, being a medical professional, can handle all aspects of care. While it's good for emergencies, when it comes to your child's development, it's essential to seek a specialized professional who understands the different dimensions of growth. Beyond academic qualifications, experience plays a crucial role in becoming an expert in our respective fields of practice.

As defined by the American Academy of Pediatrics (AAP), pediatrics is a medical specialty focused on the physical, mental, and social well-being of children from birth to early adulthood. Its primary goal is to ensure the optimal health of children.

Pediatric services cover everything from preventive care to diagnosing and treating illnesses. Additionally, pediatrics takes into account the various biological, social, and environmental factors that influence a child's development. According to the AAP, children differ from adults in several areas, such as anatomy, physiology, immunology, psychology, development, and metabolism.

For these reasons, my recommendation is clear: the initial evaluation should be conducted by a pediatrician, while respecting the importance of other medical areas as well. According to the AAP, a pediatrician is a physician who primarily focuses on the health, well-being, and development of children. Their unique qualifications come from their academic preparation and experience in this field. A pediatrician can accurately assess your child's health, act as a consultant, and collaborate with other specialists as needed.

Pediatric services are available from the moment of birth until approximately early adulthood, which is generally around the age of eighteen, varying slightly depending on the country and cultural norms.

### How often should I take my child to see the pediatrician?

I recommend taking your child to the pediatrician for preventive check-ups at least once a year. Ideally, this visit should occur during the months of June and July, prior to the start of the school year. However, if your child has been recommended any treatment, you should take them as many times as necessary within that year.

Lastly, an important piece of advice is that we, as parents or guardians, should never discharge our children from health treatments on our own. It is always the specialist, in this case, the pediatrician, who determines when it is appropriate to discharge the child from treatment.

### What can I expect during a pediatric evaluation?

A comprehensive pediatric evaluation covers both basic and complex aspects of a child's health. Different countries, represented by organizations like the Spanish Society of Out-of-Hospital and Primary Care Pediatrics and the American Academy of Pediatrics, follow the pediatric evaluation triangle model, which consists of the following three areas: appearance, respiratory effort, and skin circulation.

These areas are further divided into specific indicators, each assigned a score or value, aiming for a balanced assessment among the three. Here is a summary of these areas, which will help you better understand the evaluation results.

## Appearance

This is the first area to evaluate, and it often begins unnoticed when the pediatrician greets and interacts with the child. It is part of the initial medical assessment and greeting process.

This area includes several indicators: muscle tone, responsiveness, comfort (crying and calming), eye contact, and language. To assess muscle tone, the doctor may ask the child to perform simple tasks like lifting an arm or leg in different directions.

The second indicator, responsiveness, assesses if the child is alert to stimuli in the environment. For example, the doctor may offer a toy and observe if the child reaches out to touch it.

Comfort is another important indicator, as it's natural for the child to cry during unfamiliar situations, but the expectation is that they can be calmed afterward.

The doctor will also pay attention to eye contact, observing if the child can maintain it with people and objects. They will engage the child in conversation, assessing their ability to respond appropriately based on their age.

Language is another significant indicator. The doctor may ask the child basic questions like their name, age, or where they live to evaluate their language skills based on their developmental stage.

### Respiratory System

During this part of the evaluation, the doctor will ask you to unbutton or remove the child's shirt to observe, palpate, and listen to the chest area using their professional instruments, such as a stethoscope. The indicators they will evaluate are the breath sounds and visual signs.

Abnormal breath sounds, such as grunting, may indicate possible obstructions in the respiratory system. The doctor will also pay attention to hoarseness when the child exhales. Additionally, they will listen for any "wheezing" (a whistling or wheezing sound while breathing), which could be related to a health condition if present.

### Skin Circulation

Finally, the doctor evaluates the skin circulation, which includes the indicators of pallor and cyanosis (bluish discoloration of the skin caused by oxygenation issues in the blood). Skin color can reveal signs of certain health conditions.

Once the pediatrician assesses these three areas, they can determine if there is any imbalance and, if necessary, recommend further tests. As part of the routine evaluation, the pediatrician may request blood, urine, and stool tests, among others, as needed. It is essential to undergo these tests as they can help identify health conditions such as hypoglycemia, diabetes, thyroid problems, and others.

Identifying these conditions in a timely manner is crucial as they can negatively impact learning. Some conditions can affect mood, attention levels, and consequently, the learning process. For example, hypoglycemia, characterized by low blood sugar levels, can cause dizziness, blurred vision, tremors, nausea, crying, poor coordination, lethargy, erratic responses to questions, and headaches, among other symptoms. These symptoms can significantly affect a child's ability to pay attention to what they are reading, analyzing, and interpreting.

## Second Stop – Eye Evaluation

This second stop on the journey will take you to a specialist who evaluates your child's eyesight to ensure they are ready for learning. Remember that sight is one of the most utilized senses in the learning process, making this stop essential before proceeding to the next steps.

Vision is so crucial that "visual learners" have been identified—those who find learning easier through the use of images and graphics. For instance, in my classes, I always incorporate videos, images, and PowerPoint presentations, and the feedback I receive from students is that these visuals help them better understand the material discussed.

The most important piece of information is that approximately 65% of the population are visual learners, but even more astonishingly, for children, it can represent up to 80% of their learning. For this reason, in some regions, such as the Department of Education in the state of Kentucky, USA, before starting kindergarten, parents are asked to have their child undergo an eye examination, in addition to the physical and dental evaluations.

All of this reminded me of Lisa, who started kindergarten and her mother said she constantly fell and tripped over objects. This led to several accidents when she was younger, and even prompted an investigation to rule out abuse.

The visual examination revealed that Lisa had significant visual impairment, with a condition that could worsen and require more intensive treatment. Once Lisa's visual needs were addressed, she stopped falling and tripping, and one day she told me, "I never realized how beautiful my teacher is."

In today's technology-driven era, there are additional measures we can take to protect our children's vision. Prolonged exposure to various types of screens can lead to serious vision problems. According to the American Optometric Association and *Clarin Salud*, there is a condition known as "computer vision syndrome" that you should be aware of for the well-being of your children and your family in general.

This syndrome develops due to the effect of prolonged exposure to bright screens at a close distance. The main symptoms often include blurred vision, eye fatigue and irritation, neck pain, light sensitivity, dry eyes, double vision, dizziness, and headaches.

To prevent this syndrome, it is recommended that children not spend more than two hours in front of electronic devices, including televisions. Many modern TVs come with warnings about screen exposure and the recommended duration and distance for usage.

Education is crucial for both adults and children in this matter, especially for those under two years of age. The American Optometric Association recommends the 20-20-20 strategy, which means taking a break every twenty minutes to focus on something twenty feet away for twenty seconds, away from the electronic device.

### What Is Optometry?

The World Council of Optometry, in a report presented in 2010 to mark its 90th anniversary, included several interesting facts. I'm going to share the three that I consider most important:

- 80% of visual impairments (vision conditions) can be prevented. Refractive errors are among the top two causes of these problems.

- There are 285 million people worldwide with visual impairments and 39 million who are considered blind.
- Lastly, they state that many of these situations could be prevented with timely visual examinations.

They define this area of medicine as a profession of visual health, aimed at preventing, detecting, and solving visual problems. They pay special attention to the functioning of the visual system at short distances, such as reading, writing, and precision work, among other activities, as that's where visual problems often begin. Vision is the ability to process environmental information, give it meaning, and understand what is seen through the eyes.

According to the American Optometric Association, visual examinations are recommended at six months, three years, and before starting first grade. Afterward, an annual evaluation is recommended, ideally before the start of the school year. These early-age examinations ensure that your child is developing normally as they grow and prepare to enter school.

To measure visual acuity, the optometrist conducts evaluations and, if they identify any need, they may recommend eyeglass prescriptions. Below, I share only some of the visual conditions that can affect vision.

- **Myopia** - Characterized by blurry distance vision, myopia is one of the most common visual conditions. Having this condition would significantly impact learning, as the child wouldn't be able to recognize and identify letters and words. For example, if a psychological test is administered to a child with myopia, the results would be affected. This condition presents difficulty in seeing distant objects, headaches, and redness of the eyes.

- **Astigmatism** - Causes images to appear unclear and distorted. For example, a child may see several pictures, but can't clearly distinguish their details. Some symptoms include distorted vision, headaches, eye fatigue, and difficulty with night vision.

- **Hyperopia** - Usually manifests as blurry vision when objects are close. For instance, this would affect the child when transferring information from the chalkboard to their notebook. Symptoms may include headaches, fatigue, strabismus (crossed or squinted eyes), and burning or itching in the eyes.

## Third Stop – Audiological Evaluation

In many instances, we assume that our children hear well, or as we say in Puerto Rico, "that they hear what they want to hear." However, there are different types of hearing losses, some of which can be progressive and of a greater degree, affecting learning. That's why it's essential to conduct a preventive audiological evaluation and ensure that it's not a case of "hearing what they want to hear," but rather a hearing impairment.

I particularly recall two situations I worked with. Both were students with hearing loss that had gone unnoticed because neither of them had difficulties in speech. Difficulty in speaking is one of the most common signs of hearing loss. One of these students, Roberto, was eleven years old, and his hearing loss, though not profound, required the use of two hearing aids. Roberto's hearing needs were identified thanks to a health services fair we organized at the school.

In the other situation, it was the teacher who noticed that Valentina was sitting tilted to her right side during class, which she interpreted as a way to hear better. When we met with her mother, we explained the teacher's concern, and she mentioned that she hadn't noticed anything unusual. After making several referrals, it was identified that Valentina was born without a cochlea.

What is the cochlea, and why is it important for hearing? The cochlea, also known as the snail due to its spiral shape, is one of the internal organs of the ear. Since Valentina was missing one cochlea, she couldn't hear through that ear. Fortunately, she had hearing in the other ear, but she also had some hearing loss there.

There were different options to address the auditory diversity situation in this case. Among the possible solutions was to undergo a cochlear implant procedure or use an external device that would assist in cochlear function. However, the external device didn't appeal to Valentina's mother aesthetically, even though she was willing to consider a cochlear implant. Ironically, she didn't qualify for the cochlear implant option due to the minimal hearing loss in her other ear.

Nevertheless, a third possibility emerged, which involved providing Valentina with an electronic device that maximized her teacher's voice volume. This solution allowed us to overcome this obstacle. I must mention that this entire process took us a year or even more to finalize.

## What Is Audiology?

Audiology is the branch of medicine that studies and treats problems and conditions related to the ear, hearing, and how sounds are perceived. It also focuses on the prevention, treatment, and rehabilitation of auditory system disorders. The professional responsible for evaluating and identifying the need for hearing aids through a specialized study called audiometry is known as an audiologist.

Audiometry is a test that measures the ability to hear sound waves. Based on the results of this study, it can determine whether the hearing loss is mild, moderate, or severe, guiding the recommendation for the use of hearing aids.

Hearing loss affects between one to four out of every thousand children. We humans have binaural hearing (using both ears), which is directly linked to speech and language development. Therefore, depending on the type of hearing loss, speech and language abilities may be affected, and consequently, learning. A child listens, memorizes, and repeats. If they don't hear well, their vocabulary and overall development can be limited.

There are several signs that may indicate a child is not hearing well:

- Not noticing someone speaking to them from outside their field of vision.
- Being startled when called, regardless of the noise level.
- Preferring to sit close to the television, even if the volume is appropriate.
- Turning up the volume of the radio and television excessively.
- Struggling to distinguish voices over the phone.
- Not reacting to loud sounds.

Causes of hearing loss can be either congenital (from birth) or acquired. Acquired hearing loss can result from diseases, prenatal infections, or conditions during childbirth.

### Conductive Hearing Loss

If you notice that your child perceives sounds as lower in volume even when they are not, and they also speak loudly, it's essential to have their hearing evaluated. One possible reason for this could be the accumulation of earwax (cerumen) in the ear canal, which can be resolved by ear lavage performed by a doctor at the recommended frequency. Another potential cause could be what is known as "swimmer's ear" (external otitis), a bacterial infection that occurs when the ear remains moist after bathing or swimming.

In this type of hearing loss, there is damage to the external or middle ear, making it mostly temporary and treatable in children. The key is to address the situation promptly to prevent any long-term consequences. Regular evaluations and timely interventions can help ensure optimal hearing health for your child.

### Neurosensory Hearing Loss

Unlike the previous type, neurosensory hearing loss can be present from birth or develop through exposure to loud noises and medications that affect hearing. It is related to a malfunction of the inner ear, specifically the cochlea or the "snail" as it is called. This type of damage occurs in the inner ear, is permanent, and cannot be treated with medication or surgery in most cases. However, hearing aids and cochlear implants can be beneficial, although their effectiveness depends on each individual's specific situation. Early detection and intervention are crucial for managing and optimizing the child's hearing abilities in such cases.

### Mixed Hearing Loss

Mixed hearing loss is caused by a combination of factors that affect both the inner ear (cochlea) and the middle ear.

### Speech and Language Evaluation (if necessary)

I have had the opportunity to support many families with such needs, but I particularly remember two of them with much love and hope. Mario was five years old and already attending kindergarten. He was referred by his teacher because he stuttered.

This situation presented several challenges for him, such as frustration when trying to participate in class, as his classmates would laugh at him due to the delays in his speech. It also affected his ability to initiate the writing process, as speech difficulties can impact writing as well. We started the plan and referred him, incorporating all the steps described earlier in this book (pediatrician, visual and auditory evaluation), and added the referral for speech and language evaluation.

Unfortunately, the child did not participate in preschool, which helps identify such situations at an early age. Additionally, several family members had the same condition, and they believed that his stuttering did not require attention, as they had normalized it within the family.

To conclude the story, the child received speech therapy for six years, twice a week. This process was long and challenging, but the success became evident in Mario's later life, as he grew into a talented and highly capable young leader.

The other situation was that of a young university student in one of my classes who would stutter when she got nervous. I bring up this example to highlight the importance of early detection, so that a person doesn't carry this condition into adulthood, which could not only affect their academic performance but also their social life.

The first time it happened, it was a bit challenging for me. I called her name as it was her turn to respond to what we had discussed. When she didn't answer, and since I like to use humor in my classes, I said, "Iris, don't tell me you forgot so quickly?" To my embarrassment, it wasn't that she forgot; she got nervous and started to stutter. I became concerned when she didn't attend the next two classes, but eventually, she returned and turned out to be one of the best students in the course.

Do you notice your child feeling frustrated because others don't understand them? According to Psychology Today, one in ten children has functional diversity in the area of speech and language, making the need for therapy in this area important. Children's Healthcare of Atlanta in the United States states that speech and language therapy can help a child speak more clearly, enabling them to feel more confident and less frustrated when trying to be understood by others.

Moreover, therapy helps strengthen their social, emotional, and academic language skills. Children with difficulties in reading can improve their auditory skills and better distinguish specific sounds in words, thus enhancing their reading abilities. This therapy is highly beneficial, especially when started at an early age. Depending on the individual's needs, it can last from months to years, so it's not a quick fix.

## Who Is the Speech Pathologist and Who Is the Therapist?

The speech-language pathologist conducts the speech and language evaluation. Before conducting this evaluation on the child, they will recommend an audiological test to ensure proper hearing. According to the American Speech-Language-Hearing Association, this evaluation includes the following areas:

- **Receptive Language** - This assesses what the child understands, especially when reading a story to them. Questions may be asked to gauge the child's language comprehension.
- **Expressive Language** - This focuses on how the child communicates and if they can express themselves in complete sentences.
- **Pragmatic Language** - This examines how the child uses language socially. For example, it observes whether they make eye contact while speaking, pay attention to the teacher's instructions, and can take turns in a conversation.
- **Articulation** - This assesses how the child pronounces the sounds of the alphabet and words.
- **Oral Examination** - The therapist examines the child's facial muscles, lips, teeth, tongue, palate, and throat while eating and speaking, as all of this is linked to the speech and communication process. It is also essential to visit the dentist, as some needs can be addressed before reaching this evaluation, or the dentist may recommend it.

- **Voice** - The therapist evaluates the tone, rhythm, and volume of speech, as the child might speak hoarsely or too softly.
- **Fluency** - This evaluates the child's speech flow, ensuring that their message is expressed without major interruptions, such as stuttering, elongated sounds or words, repetition, hesitation, and fillers.
- **Feeding and Swallowing** - This area observes the child's mouth and the ability of their facial muscles to eat, suck, chew, and swallow. It also addresses their tolerance for different food textures, choking incidents, and other difficulties.

The therapist provides therapy to children once they are evaluated and the service is recommended. These professionals can help resolve language-related problems, including dyslexia (a reading disorder where they may confuse or alter the order of letters, syllables, or words) or dyspraxia (related to the lack or absence of coordinated movements, often accompanied by other verbal and neurological difficulties).

## Psychological Evaluation

Rosaura was eight years old and in second grade when we sat down with her paternal grandmother, who had custody of her since her mother had passed away at the time of her birth, to discuss the results of the psychological evaluation. She was receiving services in the special education program, including educational support and various therapies such as speech and language therapy and occupational therapy.

We conducted a reevaluation in the area of psychology, as her last evaluation had been when she was five years old, and we wanted to see if there were any changes in this area during that period. Rosaura had repeated the second grade. When I saw the diagnostic impression in the evaluation, it caused me great concern for several reasons.

Firstly, I was worried about the stigma that is sometimes associated with evaluation results, and secondly, I was concerned about how the interpretation of the results could impact the child's educational placement. The evaluation indicated that Rosaura's IQ fell within the category of "intellectual disability" under the classification of mild.

However, after carefully analyzing the situation and taking into account the observations of her teachers and some of the work she had done, we decided to establish a long-term action plan. An important point I want to share with you is that, many times, the diagnostic impression is not a final diagnosis, and with proper stimulation and support provided to the child, this can change over time.

Once we discussed the evaluation, we established a work plan to support the student, which also involved her grandmother. Despite her grandmother not knowing how to read or write, she was available and willing to collaborate and support Rosaura.

We agreed that after her regular classes, Rosaura would attend tutoring sessions at a nearby center. The center was free of charge, and her grandmother would take her there. Additionally, she received reasonable accommodations and the option of a resource room, which is part of the public education system in Puerto Rico, offering individualized help from Monday to Friday for one hour. To complete her support, she continued receiving speech therapy, occupational therapy, and psychological counseling.

This plan was implemented for two and a half years, with reviews every ten weeks. Three years later, a reevaluation in the area of psychology showed an improvement in her academic performance. When the evaluation results arrived, there was a change in the diagnostic impression. It no longer read "intellectual disability" but had been modified to "specific learning problem."

However, as the evaluation did not specify her specific learning problem, they recommended a psychoeducational evaluation. Later on, I will explain the different types of evaluations in the field of psychology, as well as other important information related to these evaluations.

## What Is Psychology?

The American Psychological Association tells us that this professional field deals with the study of the mind and behavior. It encompasses all aspects of people's experiences, considering their developmental stages. It involves understanding the behavior of children from birth to adolescence and providing necessary diagnoses and treatments during their development. This includes studying physical, motor, cognitive, perceptual, emotional, and social development.

### Types of Psychological Evaluations Available for Children

According to Dr. Marilyn Rodríguez, a clinical psychologist, there are various evaluations that can be conducted for children. Let's explore some of them:

- **Psychological evaluations** - These provide essential information about how the child functions and operates based on their chronological age and developmental expectations. In these evaluations, the child's intelligence quotient (IQ) is measured, reflecting their cognitive abilities compared to other children their age. Many times, such evaluations identify multiple needs that may require further specific tests, such as in the areas of speech and language, psychiatry, or neurology. I recall an instance where a psychological evaluation report for a girl included the following: "Referred to a psychiatrist for R/O ADHD." At that moment, I didn't understand this recommendation, but upon contacting the specialist, I learned that "R/O" stands for "rule out," indicating a need to consider the possibility of attention deficit hyperactivity disorder.

- **Psychoeducational evaluation** - This assessment aims to understand the factors and areas affecting your child's academic and school development. Similar to the psychological evaluation, it involves various methods of gathering information, including interviews with parents or guardians and completing questionnaires and tests that assess different learning areas, such as reading comprehension, auditory memory, and writing, among others. With this data, the student's profile becomes clearer and more specific, enabling the design of a specific plan in collaboration with teachers and the child's family to enhance their strengths and address areas requiring more support, such as reading or writing. At the end of the evaluation, a report is discussed and delivered.

- **Psychometric evaluations** - Through this type of assessment, the child's intellectual potential and personality can be understood. Many times, these tests are requested by educational institutions as part of the admission process to ensure that children can cope with the academic workload and curriculum they offer. I have particularly noticed their use in schools with advanced curricula that seek to group children with high IQs, as this is believed to predict academic success.

### What Should I Know About Psychological Evaluations?

Psychological tests help us understand the causes and factors behind learning problems, as these tests are further divided into more specific areas. They also provide insights into the child's psychobiological system through interviews with the mother or family member and the analysis of health documents. Based on all this information, a psychodiagnosis is established if necessary, and a help plan is prepared.

When conducting evaluations in the field of psychology, in addition to interviewing the mother, father, or caregiver, the evaluator integrates clinical observation, the use of questionnaires, and various tests selected based on what needs to be measured and the child's age. Through this process, other specific areas of need can be identified, which may require further exploration, such as speech and language, occupational therapy, and physical therapy, among others. For example, one of the most commonly used tests is the Wechsler Intelligence Scale for Children (WISC-IV), which aims to measure the intelligence or intelligence quotient of children. This test comprises verbal and performance scales, which are further divided into sub-tests that measure more specific areas.

One of these areas is verbal comprehension, which includes vocabulary, similarities, comprehension, and the child's ability to acquire and retain information, among other areas. Most of these tests are conducted over a period of time during which the child is expected to complete all the activities that are part of the evaluation.

The Wechsler test also includes the area of "working memory," which measures the child's capacity for retaining and storing information. For example, it assesses how the child uses acquired information and generates new information based on what they have learned. Lastly, it includes the area of information processing speed. This section has several sub-tests: coding, symbol search, and animal and object sorting, measuring the child's attention capacity, visual exploration, organization, and discrimination of information presented by the psychologist.

In a psychological evaluation of one of my participants, the evaluation methods or components included, in addition to the WISC, a social-emotional and developmental history of the child, clinical observations by the psychologist, the Bender Visual Motor Gestalt Test II, the Colored Progressive

Matrices (Raven's), Rorschach Inkblot Test, and the Incomplete Sentences Test, for a total of eight assessments.

Each of these tests seeks to obtain information on different areas of the child's development. For example, the Bender Visual Motor Gestalt Test II is a pencil and paper test in which the psychologist presents figures to the child and asks them to reproduce them. This assesses their visual-motor perception (eye-hand coordination skills), and although there is no time limit for this test, the time taken by the child to complete it is noted.

Depending on the results of these tests, along with the analysis of other gathered information, a referral might be made to a neurologist, occupational therapist, or both. In this case, if you ask me which one to go to first, I would recommend starting with the neurologist, as they will ensure that the child's brain areas are functioning well.

## Occupational Therapy Evaluation

When I conducted the interview with Sara's mother, she was very distressed. Both she and the teacher couldn't understand why Sara, with a high IQ at nine years old and receiving therapies, couldn't complete her written tasks. The situation was that she constantly came home with incomplete assignments because, at times, she didn't write down that she had homework and assignments to do at home, affecting her academic performance.

Sara was a child with double-exceptionality, as defined by Dr. Ana Miró, coordinator of a family, community and individual support project (AFEECTO), as "students who are talented or identified as gifted and have another exceptionality (disability)." In Puerto Rico, the Law 146 of 2018 of the Charter of Rights of the Gifted Student of Puerto Rico defines a gifted student as a child or youth with an IQ of 130 or higher.

In Sara's case, she had an IQ of 138 and had also received a diagnosis of Attention Deficit Hyperactivity Disorder (ADHD). This diagnosis came from a psychiatrist about a year earlier after several evaluations in the areas of psychology and neurology. Additionally, Sara was receiving pharmacological therapy (medications) and psychotherapy.

Upon analyzing all the evaluation documents that had been conducted on the child, we found that she had undergone occupational therapy evaluation two years ago, and it was recommended that she receive services in this area twice a week. The mother indicated that she was not clear on how this therapy would benefit her daughter's learning, especially in reading and writing, so she had postponed it for later.

We can see, then, that by not fully addressing the child's needs, they were not achieving the goal they were aiming for, which was for her to keep up with what her IQ level indicated.

### What Is Occupational Therapy?

The American Occupational Therapy Association tells us that occupational therapy is the only profession that helps people throughout their lives, starting from childhood to assist them in doing what they want and need to do through therapeutic use of daily activities. This is why their activities may seem like "play."

These activities help people of all ages live life to the fullest. Among the benefits they provide to children is enabling them to fully participate in school and social situations. Occupational therapy can also be helpful when a child experiences an injury that requires recovery to carry out age-appropriate activities. Occupational therapy services generally include individualized assessment and intervention to improve the child's quality of life in daily living and learning.

Throughout my experience, I have encountered many situations where children have not received the necessary occupational therapy for various reasons. This not only affects their development in this area but also their learning and, consequently, their future.

One of the main reasons for this deficit in therapy is a lack of understanding of its importance. For example, some mothers commented to me that occupational therapists were just "playing" with the children. They were unaware that these play activities were designed to work on specific areas of development and strengthen coordination skills, such as connecting visual input (eye) with tactile input (hand) for writing.

When conducting an assessment in this area, the goal is to determine the child's level of independence in daily tasks and their attention and task performance abilities. For instance, the development of fine motor skills in the hands for writing and manipulating objects is evaluated.

Like the previous evaluations, this assessment also includes ensuring that the child can see and hear well as they will be receiving instructions and performing tasks.

Upon completing the evaluation, a report is prepared and discussed with the person responsible for the child. If services in this area are needed, they will be directed towards strengthening the identified areas of need. From my experience, I can tell you that this is one of the most crucial areas of service to facilitate a child's learning, as it integrates all the senses in the therapeutic process.

### Who Is the Occupational Therapist?

According to the definition provided by Dr. Beatriz Matesanz García, an occupational therapist contributes their expertise to improve the compromised abilities of the child, such as correctly gripping a pencil to write, and through their services, they teach strategies that compensate and enable the child to perform the task.

These professionals, who can be found in school settings, therapeutic service centers, or independent offices, help children with difficulties related to physical coordination, organization, work capabilities, as well as some learning and attention difficulties that affect their ability to complete tasks.

To receive services in this area, the first step is to refer the child for an evaluation. This referral can originate from a psychological evaluation, as it happens in most cases, or it can be requested by you as a mother, father, or caregiver. It may also be recommended by their pediatrician, teacher, social worker, or another professional depending on the situation. Health insurers, as well as public organizations, may have specific protocols for accessing these services.

I should also mention that occupational therapy services can be provided by the therapist or their assistant, under the therapist's supervision. However, only the occupational therapist can conduct the evaluation. In these evaluations, just like in psychological and other assessments, your child will receive instructions to perform activities, and we need to ensure that they have had visual and audiological evaluations before being assessed.

## Psychiatric Evaluation

Zuleyka, an eight-year-old girl, was repeating the first grade. She lived with her mother and a younger brother. The teacher referred her to my office, as despite her learning ability, she was facing difficulties in her school performance. For instance, she had challenges in her interpersonal relationships with her peers, as she had aggressed two other girls on multiple occasions. She bit one of them and buried the tip of a pencil in the arm of another.

In both situations, we had to refer them to their respective pediatricians. Whenever a child sustains a skin injury, I always recommend that they be evaluated by this professional, in case they require any medication or treatment. This way, we prevent any further complications.

During discussions with the teacher, she mentioned that on several occasions, when she reprimanded Zuleyka, the girl would throw desks and tables, causing her classmates to be scared and reluctant to attend school. Similarly, during the interview with the mother, she tearfully shared that managing her daughter at home was challenging. There were times when she feared for the safety of her children, as Zuleyka had taken a knife on two occasions to aggress her brother during their arguments while playing. Additionally, she mentioned that Zuleyka slept very little during the nights and experienced nightmares.

The mother suspected that Zuleyka's poor sleep pattern was causing her to be in a constant bad mood. She felt frustrated as she didn't know what else to do for her daughter or which medical professional to consult, considering she was already seeing a psychiatrist.

In this situation, the girl was receiving educational support services for her Spanish and other subjects, and she had undergone several evaluations that led to her participation in active therapies: psychology, occupational therapy, speech and language therapy, and psychiatry.

She was receiving pharmacological treatment (medication) and psychotherapy from a pediatric psychiatrist. However, despite all these services, something was still missing. I often likened situations like this to solving a puzzle and asked myself, "What is the missing piece?"

That's when we decided to refer the girl to a specialist in neurodevelopment, as we lacked an answer or explanation for this situation. The problem could have been a misdiagnosis, leading to a treatment that didn't quite meet her needs. The extensive evaluation provided several recommendations, and copies were sent to her pediatric psychiatrist and all the other professionals involved in her care.

Following the evaluation, the girl's psychiatric treatment was reevaluated, and a new plan was established. Her educational plan was also redesigned to include strategies for managing her behavior during situations like those that had already occurred in both the classroom and at home. Teachers, therapists, and, of course, her mother were all involved in these plans.

These plans can take months to years to show results. I say this from experience to emphasize the importance of being persistent in these processes, which involve discipline in managing all aspects of their services and treatments.

I assure you that if you do so, you will see the results in your child's achievements. Today, this young woman is no longer on pharmacological treatment and is completing her professional studies, all thanks to her mother's determination and perseverance despite those significant stressors. She kept moving forward with her plan, and it has paid off.

### What Is a Psychiatric Evaluation?

According to the CareFirst Encyclopedia website, a comprehensive psychiatric evaluation can help diagnose emotional, behavioral, and developmental disorders in children. It is conducted based on the child's behavior during the assessment, taking into consideration physical, genetic, environmental, social, cognitive (thinking), emotional, and educational factors that may be affecting the observed behaviors.

When performing a comprehensive psychiatric evaluation in children and adolescents, it may include:

- A description of the behaviors observed during the assessment. When did they occur? How long did they last? Under what conditions do they typically occur? For example, in the case presented, we provided a report on the situations that occurred at school and at home, along with the dates of these events, among other data.

- A description of the symptoms (observable signs). In this part, for instance, we shared with the doctors the teachers' observations regarding classroom participation, interactions with other children, motivation to engage in individual and group activities, and more.

- The impact of these behaviors on school performance. In this area, with the mother's permission, we shared her grades or academic performance so that changes after receiving treatments could be analyzed.

- Relationships and interactions with others (parents, siblings, classmates, and other individuals). This information is also collected in the interview conducted by the psychiatrist with the person accompanying the child as part of the evaluation process.

- A psychiatric interview. At this stage, the psychiatrist structures the areas to be explored based on the referred data.

- A personal and family history of emotional, behavioral, or developmental disorders.

- A complete medical history that includes an overall description of the child, a list of all present illnesses or conditions, and any ongoing treatment at the time of the evaluation.

- Blood laboratory tests and radiology studies.

- Educational, speech and language, psychological evaluations, social work psychosocial history, among others.

A psychiatric evaluation is different from a psychological evaluation, as a psychiatrist, due to their professional training, focuses on integrating both the biological and psychological aspects in their analysis. To become a psychiatrist, one must first study medicine and then specialize in the field of mental health.

In addition to providing psychotherapy services, a psychiatrist is the only professional qualified to prescribe pharmacological or medication therapy to address mental health conditions, after identifying the specific needs of the participant, in this case, the child.

### Who Is the Pediatric Psychiatrist?

According to the American Academy of Child and Adolescent Psychiatry, a child and adolescent psychiatrist is a medical doctor who specializes in diagnosing and treating thought, emotional, and behavioral disorders that affect children, adolescents, and their families.

This is achieved by integrating their expertise and conducting a comprehensive evaluation, as mentioned earlier. Once the evaluation is completed, the psychiatrist can arrive at a diagnosis that is shared with the family, and then a plan is designed to address all identified needs, which are shared and integrated with the family.

An integrated treatment plan may include individual, group, or family psychotherapy, medication, or consultations with other doctors or professionals from schools, juvenile courts, social agencies, or other community organizations.

## Neurological Evaluation

Rubí was in first grade. She had silky, curly hair that covered part of her beautiful face, complemented by a warm smile, although a hint of shyness lurked behind it.

During her first grade, the girl was referred by her teacher because on several occasions, while performing tasks such as writing, reading, or even walking, she would freeze for several seconds. Although Rubí would react a few seconds later, the teacher didn't know how to help her. I had the opportunity to observe this in the classroom for several days.

When I met with Rubí's mother to discuss this concern and conducted the social history interview of the child, I discovered that she had received treatment for seizures during her early years, but they had disappeared, and the mother thought it was not necessary to continue the treatment. Furthermore, she expressed that it was a challenge for her to seek continuity in treatment, as she had tried to obtain a referral to a neurologist through the child's pediatrician, but it was impossible to get one.

Adding to the difficulties, they did not have transportation services. After completing the history, we managed to identify a non-profit organization that provided this service for free. The place was more than an hour away from their home, but we arranged transportation through the municipal administration.

When the mother met with me again after the appointment with the neurologist, she was very satisfied with the evaluation that was conducted on Rubí, as well as the recommendations given for home management and for us at the school.

According to the Centers for Disease Control and Prevention (CDC, 2018), "Epilepsy is a brain disorder that causes seizures. The way a seizure looks depends on the type the person is experiencing. Some seizures may appear as catatonic episodes," which is what happened to Rubí.

Other seizures may cause a person to fall, tremble, and not be aware of what is happening around them, as it happened to a classmate in university while studying. I remember that suddenly she fell off her chair and had many movements in her body, and after the episode ended, she started crying.

The reasons why I refer to neurologists go beyond epilepsy. I also refer for other conditions such as attention deficit hyperactivity disorder (ADHD), Tourette syndrome, autism spectrum disorder, speech and language issues, among others. As each situation is unique, the plan of action follows different routes based on the analysis of the child's needs.

### What Is a Neurological Evaluation?

I'm going to return to Joselo's situation. This student had several visits with his pediatrician where problems with blood, thyroid, and even hearing were evaluated. With the support of a specialized pediatric neurologist, it was discovered that Joselo had what is known as an epileptic absence seizure.

It was something that none of us had initially considered, and precisely this was what was affecting his learning. Additionally, he also had hypoglycemia (low blood sugar).

To reach this diagnosis, and eventually a follow-up treatment, several visits to the doctor and many tests were required. Finally, it was the pediatric neurologist who was able to uncover the root of the problem. The contribution of the child's mother was a very important element, as she followed the recommendations and remained consistent, enabling her son to improve this condition until it eventually disappeared in adolescence. So remember, you are one of the most important pieces of this puzzle. We need you!

### What Can I Expect From a Neurological Evaluation?

During a neurological evaluation, similar to previous assessments, you will be asked to complete certain documents providing information about the child and family health history, among other details. Additionally, you will participate in an interview to provide more specific reasons for the referral. As part of the assessment process, these specialized doctors in the nervous system can arrive at their diagnoses by gathering information about symptoms, medical history, and conducting a physical examination.

However, to ensure more accurate diagnoses, they may request certain specialized tests depending on the need. Occasionally, these tests can be quite costly, and they may ask you to pay a portion or even the full cost in advance. Check with a social worker who can assist you in identifying organizations that offer these services at a lower cost or sometimes even for free. For example, in Joselo's situation, all neurological services were provided free of charge.

1. **Electroencephalogram (EEG)** - This test aims to identify issues in the brain's electrical activity. It can help detect various types of seizures in children.
2. **Magnetic Resonance Imaging (MRI) or Computed Tomography (CT) Scan** - This study captures images of the brain or spinal cord and can help identify tumors, strokes, infections, multiple sclerosis, and other genetic conditions.
3. **Lumbar Puncture** - In this test, a small needle is inserted into the lower back to obtain a small sample of cerebrospinal fluid surrounding the brain and spinal cord.

### Who Is the Pediatric Neurologist?

The pediatric neurologist is a doctor who treats children with issues related to the nervous system. The nervous system consists of two parts: the central nervous system, which includes the brain and spinal cord, and the peripheral nervous system, made up of nerve fibers branching from the spinal cord and extending to various parts of the body, including the neck, arms, torso, legs, and muscles, among other areas.

The brain sends messages through the spinal cord and the peripheral nervous system to control muscle movement and the function of other organs. This message is relayed through neurons, the cells found in the brain of which we have around 100 million. These neurons communicate with one another until the message reaches its destination to trigger an action. However, if this message is not transmitted correctly, it could lead to what happened to Joselo: the message is disrupted and fails to reach its intended target.

These doctors frequently diagnose, treat, and manage various areas, such as seizures, epilepsy, and muscle problems that can cause weakness, like muscular dystrophy and neuropathy. They also address behavioral conditions, including attention deficit with or without hyperactivity, nervous tics, Tourette's syndrome, sleep disorders, and even autism. Moreover, they handle issues related to child development, cerebral palsy, speech delays, brain tumors, infections, or inflammation of the brain, such as meningitis.

Undoubtedly, this resource is highly significant for the health and well-being of children. If an evaluation is recommended for your child, be sure to follow through and clarify any doubts you may have. Similarly, I encourage you to continue expanding your knowledge in the field of neurology, as it is essential for your child's learning. There's a field of study called "neuroscience" that might interest you, so go ahead and explore!

# Annexes

# Annex 1:
# How a Social Worker Helps You Discover Your Child

I'd like to share a bit about the profession of social work based on my training and experience working with families, and especially with children. Social work is a profession that emerged from the need for dedicated professionals advocating for human rights and social justice, aiming to facilitate change and transformation in various situations that impact daily life.

In educational settings, social work identifies how social problems or situations affect the children's ability to learn. The profession of social work was established in the 1930s in our country. In Puerto Rico, for instance, schools became significant settings to address not only children's needs but also those of the entire family and community.

We work alongside families to identify and enhance children's capacities through early recognition and attention to personal, familial, and environmental circumstances. These circumstances, if negative, can prevent them from achieving their expectations of success, both academically and socially.

According to the Department of Social Work at the University of Puerto Rico, "social work is a practice-based profession and an academic discipline that promotes social change and development, social cohesion, and the empowerment and liberation of people. Principles of social justice, human rights, collective responsibility, and respect for diversity are fundamental to social work. Supported by social work theories, social sciences, humanities, and indigenous knowledge, social work engages individuals and structures to address life challenges and enhance well-being."

On the other hand, the School Social Work Association of America defines professionals providing services in school settings as follows: "School social workers provide evidence-based mental, behavioral, and social health services. [...]. School social workers collaborate with school and community resources to help students reach their fullest potential."

To practice social work, academic training is required, typically with at least a bachelor's degree in social work, a state-issued license, and membership with the Social Worker's Guild. Additionally, we adhere to a code of ethics that guides our professional actions with participants.

For instance, we uphold the right to self-determination, which in social work refers to each individual's right to choose their own life path. Also, our professional actions are based on the principle of confidentiality, meaning that information obtained during our work belongs to the participant, and access to it is ensured through prior authorization established with the participant or their family.

To me, working with children in social work demands love, abundant empathy, and a strong commitment to providing support and companionship over time, aiming to empower the child to strengthen their capacities and achieve independent daily living.

## What Does a Social Worker Do for You?

Social workers are usually the professionals who welcome families when they are facing issues with their children, which is why we bear the responsibility of understanding all the information that helps us grasp the problem and establish an effective plan to address it. We begin our services with a referral, which can come from the family themselves or from other professionals.

As part of our work, we listen to the family's concerns through an interview, and then gather information in a document we call a history. This history can have different structures depending on the place where we work. However, there are certain areas that will always be present. For example:

- **Child's Sociodemographic Data** - Name, date of birth, age, family unit.
- **Prenatal Data** - Here, we request information from the moment the mother becomes pregnant until the child's birth, including physical and mental health situations, hospitalizations, and family circumstances, among other aspects.
- **Data from the First Year of Life until the Interview** – Here, we direct our questions to understand the child's development throughout their life in different areas: family, school, community.
- **Child's Personal Characteristics** – Typically, we provide examples from a list of characteristics where they can identify those that distinguish the child most of the time, such as "cooperative," as they assist with daily

tasks. This relates to interpersonal relationships with family and others.

- **Relationships Between Child and Family** - We're interested in understanding the relationship between the child and their family members, as well as their overall environment.

As part of this data collection process, we can visit the children's homes to understand their family environment and conduct a more comprehensive analysis. Additionally, we can incorporate techniques like drawing, photo analysis, observation, play, and incomplete sentence tests, among other strategies.

Once we have gathered the necessary data, we analyze all this information together with the family to identify the issue and its underlying causes, and establish an action plan. Throughout this process, specific actions are carried out, including referrals, coordination of community services, family meetings, and case discussions, among other activities. The duration of the plans, while structured within a predetermined timeframe with the family, depends on the child's needs.

## Annex 2:
## Development History

The professionals working with your child will conduct an initial interview. It's important to be aware of the information that may be requested during that initial visit in order to create what we call a child development history. On occasions, I've encountered situations where the mother has all the details, but it's the father or grandmother who brings the child, and this can affect this part of the assessment.

My recommendation is for the person attending the interview to review this list to ensure they have the necessary information. It's also important to check if any documentation needs to be brought along, such as a birth certificate, utility bills (water or electricity), income evidence, health insurance, assessments from other professionals, among others.

**Basic Child Information:**
- Full name of the child (including last name and any middle name)
- Date of birth (day, month, and year)
- Gender
- Name of the school the child attends or whether they receive homeschooling
- Grade or educational alternative
- Name of the teacher (if applicable)

**Family Information:**
- Name of:
  - Father
  - Mother
- Legal guardians (if the child is under their legal custody, bring the document or a copy of it)
- Mailing address
- Residential address
- Home phone number
- Mother's occupation
- Mother's work phone number
- Father's occupation
- Father's work phone number
- Email address of the responsible person

**Referral (if applicable):**
- Name of the person or professional making the referral
- Relationship to the child (e.g., social worker, teacher, pediatrician, etc.)
- Reason for referral - Why is the child being referred? What observations led to the referral?
- Parent/guardian expectations of the evaluation - How do they expect the evaluation to address their child's needs?

**Child's Health Information:**
- Child's pediatrician: name, address, and phone numbers. If you have their business card, bring it on the day of the visit.
- Information about other doctors providing services (e.g., pulmonologist, gastroenterologist, etc.)

Diagnoses: If you have them in a document provided by the doctor, it's even better to bring a copy.

## Family Information:
- Caregivers
- Primary language
- Names, ages, and relationships of all individuals living in the same household (siblings, aunts, etc.)

## Family Health and Mental Health History:
- Any family members with physical health issues? (Diabetes, high blood pressure, hypothyroidism, cancer, etc.)
- Family member with mental health issues: depression, bipolar disorder, ADHD, autism, others
- Are they receiving treatment? (If the answer to the previous question is yes)

## Prenatal and Neonatal History:
- List of medications taken during pregnancy and the reason
- Health conditions during pregnancy
- Hospitalizations
- Duration of pregnancy
- Accidents
- Length of pregnancy in weeks
- Premature birth
- Any hospitalization at birth
- General health status at birth

**Child's First Year History:**
- When did the child start crawling?
- When did they roll over?
- When did they start walking?
- When did they first smile?
- At what age did they start using the bathroom on their own?

**Health Status:**
- Surgeries
- Hospitalizations
- Accidents
- Type of feeding
- Sleep patterns
- Behavior
- Relationships with family and friends

**Emergency Contact Person:**
- Name
- Phone number
- Relationship
- Address

## Annex 3:
## IDEA

The *Individuals with Disabilities Education Act* (IDEA) defines and identifies categories of disabilities under which children are entitled to receive a free and appropriate public education. These services are provided in the states and territories of the United States, including Puerto Rico. These educational services include related services (such as psychological, physical, speech, and language therapy) according to your child's needs.

These services are provided through an early intervention system (for example, in Puerto Rico, they are available in all pediatric centers within the Department of Health regions, and they are free). This system may be managed by the State Department of Health or another department such as the Department of Education.

If you are a parent and would like to learn more about early intervention services in your state, including how to request a free evaluation for your child, consider some of the following suggestions:

- Ask your child's pediatrician for information about the early intervention system in your community or region.
- Contact the pediatrics department at a local hospital and inquire about where to call to learn more about early intervention services in your area.

For children and youth aged three to twenty-one years old, special education services and what are known as related services (such as therapies, among others) are provided through the public school system. To learn more about these services, please call your local public school. The school will provide you with information about special education policies in your area or may refer you to a district or county office where you can find this information.

If you are a parent or guardian and believe that your child may need special education and related services, be sure to inquire about how you can have your child evaluated under IDEA to determine eligibility. Often, there are materials available to inform parents about local and state policies for receiving special education and related services.

**Annex 4:**
**My *AprendÉxito* Table**

**Start Date:** _____

| Roads | Steps for Parents or Guardians | Progress Notes |
|---|---|---|
| **Road 1: Identify the geographic point**<br><br>• Where is your child currently located?<br>• Have you been offered a referral?<br>• Do you have any concerns? | **Step 1: Referral or Concern**<br>• Referred by a professional<br>• Is it your request, or a family member's?<br>**Step 2: Organize the File and Add Information**<br>• Organize your file with all available documents<br>• School-related<br>• Medical<br>• Preschool<br>• Others<br>• Developmental milestone tasks from chapter 1<br>• History<br>**Step 3: Analyze and Write What You Understand to Be the Problem or Concern** | |

141

**Road 2: Start the AprendÉxito Way**
• Where do I start?

**Step 1: Universal Stops**
• Pediatric evaluation
• Audiological evaluation
• Eyesight evaluation

**Step 2: Analyze the route**
• What were the outcomes?
• Route evaluations + existing information

**Road 3: Analyze the AprendÉxito route taken**
• What did you discover on the universal route?
• What do you still don't understand?
• What are the strengths?
• What are the areas or developing abilities that require more attention?

**Step 1: Analyze and Respond**
• What has happened since the child was evaluated? Compare to the present.
• What did I find along the universal route?
• What were the recommendations?
• Were referrals made for other evaluations or therapies?
• Were professionals recommended for these new services?
• Was I able to clarify doubts with the evaluating professionals?
• Is there still something that remains unclear to me?
• What are my child's strengths?
• What do I still don't understand or find unclear?
• What are the areas or capabilities still in development?
• Which areas require priority?

**Step 2: Decision Making**
• Option 1: Finish the journey
• Option 2: Continue the route

**Road 4: Outline Your Personal AprendÉxito Way**
- Plot your route on the map
- Begin your journey and reach the end of the route
- Evaluate the outcomes at each stop and analyze what the next step should be

**Step 1: Identify and Write**
- What are the recommendations?

**Step 2: Establish the Goal Plan**
Answer these questions:
- What do I want to achieve?
- Why do I want to achieve it?
- How am I going to achieve it?

**Step 3: Assign a Value**
- Which stop should I make first?
- Was I recommended to make one stop before another?

**Step 4: Identify and Coordinate**
- Identify potential professionals for these referrals
- Coordinate the services

**Set Short-Term Priorities (1-3 months)**
- Coordinate recommended evaluations and services, which may include:
  - Psychological evaluation
  - Speech and Language evaluation
  - Occupational therapy evaluation
  - Neurological evaluation

**History Annex**
- Verify the history annex to know what information may be asked by the evaluating professionals.

**Set Medium and Long-Term Priorities**
- School follow-up
- Follow up on therapies and re-evaluations
- Others

**Road 5: Endpoint of the *AprendÉxito* Way**
- What was the outcome?
- Do you need to repeat any stops?

**Step 1: Evaluate the paths and stops**
- Analyze the results of your goal
  - Compare the changes before and after
  - Talk to the teachers, therapists and others, and ask them about their observations
  - Depending on your child's progress, you can identify new recommendations to integrate into your plan

**Step 2: Next Step**
- Now what?
- If everything is resolved, you reached the end of your route
- Sometimes you may need to return to one of the stops, but it could be a short stop

**You can do this!**

# Glossary

**Functional Diversity** - This term offers an alternative to "disability" and highlights that each individual possesses specific abilities that need to be managed or developed (as early as possible), to prevent exclusions or discrimination when they engage with the educational and social systems.

**DSM** - The Diagnostic and Statistical Manual of Mental Disorders, published by the American Psychiatric Association, serves as a reference or guide for many professionals in diagnosing these disorders.

**Formal Education** - This intentional, planned, and regulated education consists of a set of studies that are structured and organized as part of an educational system. Primary, secondary, and university education fall under this category. It's the type of education considered mandatory up to certain levels and is overseen by the state or government.

**Informal Education** - This education occurs naturally in our daily lives without formal planning, often acquired through family, community, and various frequented places. It's a process where we learn from one another.

**Non-formal Education** - Similar to formal education, this intentional and planned education doesn't fall under the umbrella of compulsory or institutionalized schooling. It encompasses continuing education courses and home education for children who don't attend school, also known as homeschooling, among other instances.

**Developmental Milestones** - These are the expected achievements that most children should reach at a specific stage. The CDC provides various examples of milestones in areas such as social and emotional development, speech and communication, cognitive abilities, as well as motor and physical development.

**Genetic Conditions** - These are conditions that are passed down through family genes and can be inherited.

**Attention Deficit** - This is a persistent pattern of inattention and hyperactivity-impulsivity that interferes with functioning or development. It's a neurological disorder that can be categorized, based on evaluation results, as combined presentation, predominantly inattentive presentation, or predominantly hyperactive-impulsive presentation. This classification depends on the assessment conducted by a neurologist or psychiatrist.

**Autism** - This is a neurodevelopmental disorder characterized by difficulties in social interaction and communication, as well as restricted and repetitive patterns of behavior, interests, or activities. Some criteria for identifying autism include:

- Persistent communication and social interaction deficits across various contexts.
- Restrictive and repetitive behavior, interests, or activities.
- Symptoms causing significant impairment in social, educational, or other important areas.

**Social Work** - It is the profession that emerges in response to the need for dedicated professionals who advocate for human rights and social justice, aiming to facilitate change and transformation in various situations that impact people's daily lives.

**School Social Worker** - The School Social Work Association of America defines it as follows: "School social workers are authorized and certified mental health providers who serve diverse student, family, school, and community groups. They provide evidence-based mental, behavioral, and social health services. They promote safe and equitable school climate and culture, supporting positive academic and behavioral outcomes. School social workers collaborate with school and community resources to help students reach their fullest potential." For the purpose of this book, I define it as a certified sub-specialty professional working in school settings, focused on facilitating students' empowerment through enhancing their maximum potential. This involves collaboration with school staff, families, and other professionals.

**Epilepsy** - It is a disorder of the central nervous system characterized by unexpected and spontaneous seizures, triggered by excessive electrical activity in the brain.

# References

- American Academy of Child and Adolescent Psychiatry. (2015). Accessed from https://www.aacap.org/AACAP/Families_and_Youth/Facts_for_Families/FFF-Spanish/El-Psiquiatra-de-Niños-y-Adolescentes-Psiquiatra-Infantil-000.aspx

- Ápice, Asociación Andaluza de Epilepsia. ¿Qué es la epilepsia? Accessed from https://www.apiceepilepsia.org/que-es-la-epilepsia/que-es-la-epilepsia-definicion/

- ASISA. (2016). El blog de ASISA. Diferencias entre miopía, hipermetropía, astigmatismo y presbicia. Accessed from http://www.blogdeasisa.es/salud/diferencias-miopia-hipermetropia-astigmatismo-presbicia/#prettyPhoto

- American Speech-Language-Hearing Association. Speech Sound Disorders. Accessed from https://www.asha.org/public/speech/disorders/Speech-Sound-Disorders/

- American Optometric Association. (2019). ¿Qué es un doctor en optometría? Accessed from https://www.aoa.org/about-the-aoa/what-is-a-doctor of optometry

- American Psychological Association. (2019). Frequently asked questions about the American Psychology Association. Accessed from https://www.apa.org/support/about-apa

- American Ocupational Therapy Association. (2019). ¿Qué es terapia ocupacional? Accessed from https://www.aota.org/Conference-Events/OTMonth/what-is-OT.aspx

- Burgos Ortiz, N. (1998). Pioneras de la profesión en trabajo social en Puerto Rico. Editorial Publicaciones Puertorriqueñas. Accessed from http://www.ts.ucr.ac.cr/binarios/libros/libros-000040.pdf

- Centers for Disease Control and Prevention (CDC). U.S. Department of Health and Human Services. (2009). Aprenda los signos. Reaccione pronto. Accessed from https://www.cdc.gov/ncbddd/actearly/pdf/other-lang/LTSAE-SPN-Checklist-with-Tips-5anos-P.pdf

- Centers for Disease Control and Prevention (CDC). (2014). Aplying the Knowledge to Action (K2A) Framework: Questions to Guide Planning. Accessed from https://www.cdc.gov/chronicdisease/pdf/K2A-Framework-6-2015.pdf

- Centers for Disease Control and Prevention (CDC). (2018). Epilepsia. Accessed from https://www.cdc.gov/epilepsy/spanish/basicos/datos.html

- Colegio de Profesionales del Trabajo Social de Puerto Rico. (2017). Código de Ética Profesional.

- Children's Healthcare of Atlanta. Evaluación del habla y lenguaje de su niño. Accessed from https://www.choa.org/~/media/files/Childrens/medical-services/rehabilitation/outpatient-rehab/what-to-expect-speech-spanish.pdf?la=en

- Chugani, H.T. (2017). KidsHealth from Nemours. Crisis de ausencia por epilepsia en la infancia. Accessed from https://kidshealth.org/es/parents/childhood-absence-epilepsy-esp.html

- Clarín Salud. (2019). La salud de los ojos. ¿Qué es el "síndrome de visión informática? Accessed from https://www.clarin.com/salud/sindrome-vision-informatica-ojos-vision-vista-mirar-pantallas-television-computadora-lcd-tablet-smartphone-celular-tableta-dispositivos-electronicos-salud-cuidados_0_Bk-7KAtvmg.html

- World Council of Optometry. (2013). Celebración de los 90 años. Accessed from https://worldcouncilofoptometry.info/wp-content/uploads/2017/03/WCO-Presentation-FINAL-Spanish-Version.pdf

- Departamento de Trabajo Social. (2017). Universidad de Puerto Rico, Recinto de Rio Piedras. Accessed from https://sociales.uprrp.edu/trabajo-social/

- Deusto Salud. (2019). El concepto de discapacidad. Accessed from https://www.deustosalud.com/blog/ teleasistencia-dependencia/concepto-discapacidad-di-ferencias-entre-discapacidad-deficiencia

- CareFirst Encyclopedia. (2019). Evaluación psiquiátrica integral en niños. Accessed from http://carefirst. staywellsolutionsonline.com/Spanish/Encyclope-dia/90,P05674

- Esteban, E. (2019). Guía Infantil. Tabla del desarrollo de los niños de 0 a 6 años. Accessed from https://www. guiainfantil.com/articulos/bebes/desarrollo/tabla-del-desarrollo-de-los-ninos-de-0-a-6-anos/

- Estremera Jimenez, R. (2015). Trabajo Social Comunitario Puertorriqueño: De la experiencia histórica hacia un modelo liberador. Publicaciones Gaviota.

- Eunice Kennedy Shriver National Institute of Health and Human Development. (2013). ¿Cuales son las partes del sistema nervioso? Accessed from https://www1. nichd.nih.gov/espanol/salud/temas/neuro/informacion/ Pages/partes.aspx

- Fundación (CADAH). (2012). TDAH: Instrumentos o pruebas para evaluar la capacidad intelectual (CI). Accessed from https://www.fundacioncadah.org/web/ar-ticulo/tdah-instrumentos-o-pruebas-para-evaluar-la-ca-pacidad-intelectual-ci.html

- Gobierno de Puerto Rico. (2017). Departamento de Estado. Junta Examinadora de Trabajo Social. Profesionales de trabajo social. Accessed from https://www.estado.pr.gov/es/profesionales-del-trabajo-social/

- Healthy children.org (2019). ¿Qué es un neurólogo infantil? Accessed from https://www.healthychildren.org/Spanish/family-life/health-management/pediatric-specialists/Paginas/what-is-a-child-neurologist.aspx

- Horeczko, T. (2013). The Pediatric Assessmente Triangle: Accuracy of its Application by Nurses in the Triage of children. National Library of Medicine. Accessed from https://www.ncbi.nlm.nih.gov/pmc/articles/PMC4318552/

- Jesuïtes educació. (2018). Actualidad: Educación no formal, informal y formal ¿en qué consiste cada una? Accessed from https://fp.uoc.fje.edu/blog/educacion-no-formal-informal-y-formal-en-que-consiste-cada-una/

- Kentucky Department of Education. (2019). Kentucky Public School Enrollment. Requirements. Accessed from https://education.ky.gov/comm/newtoKY/Pages/Kentucky-Enrollment-Requirements.aspx

- KidsHealth from Nemours (2017). Crisis de ausencia por epilepsia en la infancia. Accessed from https://kidshealth.org/es/parents/childhood-absence-epilepsy-esp.html

- Kübler-Ross, Elisabeth. (1970, c1969) On death and dying. New York: Collier Books/Macmillan

- Lens Crafters. (2019). ¿Por qué los exámenes de la vista son importantes? Ojos saludables: La importancia de los exámenes de la vista. Accessed from https://es.lenscrafters.com/lc-us/vision-guide/eye-exams

- LexJuris Puerto Rico. (2019). Ley 146 de 2018, Carta de Derechos del Estudiante Dotado de Puerto Rico. Accessed from http://www.lexjuris.com/lexlex/Leyes2018/lexl2018146.htm

- Matesanz Garcia, B. (2008). Terapia ocupacional en el ámbito escolar. Universidad Rey Juan Carlos. Revista de Terapia Ocupacional Galcia. TOG (A. Coruña). ISSN 1885-527X. Recuperado de www.revistatog.com

- Medline Plus. Información de salud para usted. (2019). Sibilancias. Accessed from https://medlineplus.gov/spanish/ency/article/003070.htm

- MH Magazine Wordpress. (2019). Etapas de la niñez. Accessed from https://eldesarrollocognitivo.com/desarrollo-humano/etapa-de-la-ninez/

- Miró, A. Apoyo a la Familia, Estudiantes, Escuelas y Comunidad. Opusculo de la oficina de AFEECTo de la Universidad de Puerto Rico, Recinto de Rio Piedras.

- Organización Mundial de la Salud. (2013). Salud ocular universal: Un plan de acción mundial para

2014-2019. Accessed from https://www.who.int/blindness/AP2014_19_Spanish.pdf?ua=1

• National Core for Neuroethics. University of British Columbia Hospital. The Knowledge to Action Cycle. Accessed from http://dementiakt.ca/dkt-learning-centre/introduction-to-kt/kt-frameworks/

• Oficina de Vida Independiente de Andalucía. (2019). Diversidad vs discapacidad. Accessed from https://viandalucia.org/diversidad-vs-discapacidad/

• Organización Panamericana de la Salud. (2011). Implementación del modelo biopsicosocial para la atención de personas con discapacidad a nivel nacional. Oficina Regional de la Organización Mundial de la Salud.

• Phonak Life is On. Pérdida auditiva en niños. Accessed from https://www.phonak.com/es/es/perdida-auditiva/perdida-auditiva-en-ninos/signos-y-causas-niños.html

• Proyecte Autisme La Garriga. (2016). Criterios diagnosticos del autismo y el trastorno del espectro autista. Accessed from https://www.autismo.com.es/autismo/criterios-diagnosticos-del-autismo.html

• Psicodiagnosis. (2019). Evaluación psicológica. Accessed from https://www.psicodiagnosis.es/areaespecializada/evaluacionpsicologica/index.php

- Psychology Today. (2019). Communication Disorders. Accessed from https://www.psychologytoday.com/us/conditions/communication-disorders

- Rodríguez, M. (2017). Diferencias entre: Evaluación psicométrica, psicológica y psicoeducativa. Accessed from https://dra-marilyn-rodriguez-psicologia-clinica.webnode.es/l/diferencias-entre-evaluacion-psicometrica-psicologica-y-psicoeducativa/#

- School Social Work Association of America. Accessed from https://www.sswaa.org

- SINEWS. Tests psicoeucativos. Accessed from https://www.sinews.es/es/psicologia-infantil/tests-psicoeducativos.html

- Shire Pharmaceuticals Iberica S.L. Manual para diagnosticar el TDAH: DSM5. Accessed from http://www.tdahytu.es/manual-para-diagnosticar-el-tdah-dsm-5/

- UNICEF. (2018). Convención sobre los derechos del niño. Accessed from https://www.unicef.es/causas/derechos-ninos/convencion-derechos-ninos

- Villar- Epifanio, V. (2019). Diario 16, el diario de la Segunda Transición. Consecuencias de la utilización de diversidad funcional. Accessed from https://diario16.com/consecuencias-de-la-utilizacion-del-termino-diversidad-funcional/

- Wolff, H. (2012). Manual de Asesoramiento Escolar para Familias. Accessed from http://www.jdrf.org/lincoln/wp-content/uploads/sites/25/2017/08/Spanish-Resource-SAT.pdf

- Woodward Spanish. Los cinco sentidos, ciencias naturales. Accessed from https://www.spanish.cl/ciencias-naturales/cinco-sentidos.htm

- Zuñiga Velasco, R. (2014). Triangulo de evaluación pediátrica. Pediatría Integral. Accessed from https://www.pediatriaintegral.es/publicacion-2014-06/triangulo-de-evaluacion-pediatrica/

# Author's Biography

Dr. Nancy Viana Vázquez holds a bachelor's and master's degree in social work with a specialization in families, as well as a doctorate in education with a specialization in educational administration and supervision. With over twenty years of experience working with children and families in school and healthcare settings, she is a dedicated professional. She has been actively involved in higher education institutions, teaching both graduate and undergraduate programs in social work and education at institutions such as Universidad Central de Bayamón; Sistema Universitario Ana G. Méndez, Gurabo campus; Universidad Interamericana; and the University of Puerto Rico, Río Piedras campus (UPRRP).

Currently serving as an assistant professor and academic advisor at the Department of Social Work at UPRRP, Dr. Viana Vázquez is also a valuable member of the interdisciplinary team at the Faculty of Education's Double Exceptionality Project. She contributed as a workshop leader to the Alcanza Project of the Educational Research Center at the University of Puerto Rico, which integrates standards and best practices for early childhood education.

With a dedication to learning and innovation, Dr. Viana Vázquez embarked on a study of the educational systems in Finland and Sweden, which led to a professional publication at the University of Arizona. Notably, she designed the Social Work and Art project aimed at enhancing the socio-emotional learning of school-age children. In recognition of its innovation and potential benefits, the International Association for Social Work with Groups (IASWG) granted its endorsement and financial support through the SPARC Program in 2019.

She served as a school social worker, a teaching facilitator in social work, a program director, and an assistant principal in the Puerto Rico Department of Education. She provided workshops for newly qualified social work professionals during their first year of experience and offered technical assistance, guidance, and consultation to school social workers, teachers, professional counselors, principals, and superintendents.

Within the Puerto Rico Board of Professional Social Work, she is a member of the Editorial Board for the peer-reviewed journal "*Voces desde el Trabajo Social*" (Voices from Social Work) and a member of the Board of Directors for the Institute of Continuing Education. Additionally, she conducts workshops, conferences, and training sessions for both public and private organizations, catering to diverse groups including social work professionals, professional counselors, educators from higher education institutions, teachers, and personnel from preschool centers.

As part of her career responsibilities, Dr. Viana is an expert in family cases for the Puerto Rico Court Administration. She provides consulting, mentoring, workshops, and training to various professionals in social and educational fields. Her areas of expertise encompass group work, student retention, functional diversity, and dual exceptionalities, among others.